Picture *The Quiet Man*

An Illustrated Celebration

This book is dedicated to all who made it possible including my wife Anne and my family, J.J. Bunyan, Cormac O'Malley, Anne O'Maille, Charlie Harold, Grace Duncan, Gerry Cloherty, Larry McCallister, Carol Farrelly, Paddy Rock, Liam O'Raghallaigh, Gary McEwan, Aidan O'Carroll and many, many others.

First published in hardback in 2004 by
Appletree Press Ltd
The Old Potato Station
14 Howard Street South
Belfast
BT7 1AP

Tel: +44 (0) 28 9024 3074
Fax: +44 (0) 28 9024 6756
E-mail: reception@appletree.ie
Web Site: www.appletree.ie

This edition published in 2009

A catalogue record for this book is available from the British Library.

Picture *The Quiet Man*

Hardback ISBN: 978-0-86281-930-9
Paperback ISBN: 978-1-84758-143-3

Desk and Marketing Editor: Jean Brown
Designer: Stuart Wilkinson
Production Manager: Paul McAvoy

9 8 7 6 5 4 3

AP3646

Photographic credits:

© *The Connacht Tribune* (pp 5, 59, 83, 90, 92, 102, 103, 104, 105,116, 124, 125, 150)

Picture *The Quiet Man*

An Illustrated Celebration

Des MacHale

Appletree Press

Acknowledgements

I wish to express my sincerest thanks to the following for information, materials, photographs, help and encouragement.

My wife Anne, my children Peter, Catherine, Simon, John and Dominic and my mother-in-law Jane Gryce, who have helped in so many ways; Maureen O'Hara and her angelic daughter Bronwyn Fitzsimons; Charles J. Harold and Liam O'Raghallaigh, friends as well as researchers; the Farrelly family; Grace Duncan; Paddy Rock; the staff of the *Connacht Tribune* newspaper; Larry McCallister of Paramount Pictures; Gary McEwan; David McGreene; Deirdre Lydon and family; Sean Teegan; Margaret and Gerry Collins; Chris Hitchcock; Fr. Benny MacHale; Philomena O'Hara; J.J. Bunyan; June Beck; Aidan O'Carroll; Lady Killanin and family; Anne and Gerard O'Máille; the management of Ashford Castle; Harry Carey Jr; Cormac O'Malley; John Daly; Brian Downes; Luke Gibbons; Jack Murphy; Nancy Murphy; Paddy McCormick; Bill Maguire; Maura Byrne; Marian Finucane and RTE; John Cocchi; Simon Rose; Monsignor Joseph Maguire; Mike P. Ó Conaola; Ken Jones; David Quinlan; Jack Dewesberry; Neil Prenderville; Sue and Peter Ross and the many *Quiet Man* fans, too numerous to mention, who e-mailed me, phoned me and wrote to me.

CONTENTS

Introduction

One of the (few) complaints I received about my earlier book *The Complete Guide To The Quiet Man* (Appletree Press 2000) was that it didn't contain enough photographs of the stars and locations and movie stills. In this book I have put together as many photographs as I can lay my hands on; acquired through the generosity of many friends and the benevolent co-operation of several agencies, newspapers and corporations who control the copyright for reproduction of these precious images.

Some of the photographs were taken by amateurs with their box cameras on location and therefore perhaps lack the clarity and the quality of those taken by professionals; however, it is hoped that these pictures are worthy of inclusion because of their spontaneity and intrinsic interest. To those kind and generous people who donated them to me, I offer my undying thanks.

A book devoted entirely to photographs can be monotonous, so I decided that I would intersperse the book with a number of short chapters developing themes that had either been neglected or been given short measure in *The Complete Guide to the Quiet Man* – much new and serious information about the movie has come to light since 2000. Since then Cork University Press has published Luke Gibbons' *The Quiet Man* and Gerry McNee's *In the Footsteps of the Quiet Man* has been reissued by Mainstream. In addition, two monumental biographies of John Ford by Joe McBride and Scott Eyman have appeared and Maureen O'Hara's long-awaited biography *'Tis Herself* has just hit the shops – truly a wonderful time to be a 'quiet maniac'!

I have indulged myself in writing a prequel to *The Quiet Man* about what exactly might have happened before Sean Thornton arrived in Inisfree and what might have happened after Sean and Mary Kate crossed those stepping-stones over the brook to live happily ever after. These are not meant to be taken seriously but I have tried to keep them at least consistent with the action of the movie. If anybody wishes to film them, I am open to offers.

It seems that the *Quiet Man* "industry" in films, videos, DVDs, CDs, documentaries, books, replicas, re-enactments, pictures and stills and other souvenirs is increasing, rather than diminishing. *The Quiet Man* is now one of Ireland's greatest tourist attractions. Long may it continue!

Chapter One

The Quiet Boy - Sean Thornton's Story - A Prequel to The Quiet Man

May Thornton turned the key in the door of White O'Morning for what she knew would be the last time. It was a lovely cottage, with the brook flowing gently at the bottom of the garden; all around the whitewashed walls, the roses, her pride and joy, grew in great profusion. The late summer sun, just rising, threw the morning shadows of the trees across the roof of the cottage thatched with golden straw. Nostalgically, May took one last peek through the little front window – inside, everything was as neat and tidy as it always had been. The floors were so clean and scrubbed you could have eaten your dinner off them. Her one ambition was to have a casement looking out over the brook so she could see and hear it as she went about her work, singing and often dancing for sheer joy. But that never came about and now she knew it never would happen.

At White O'Morning May Thornton had for a time found true happiness. She was born May Feeney near the Céide Fields in North Mayo and had met her husband-to-be, Mike Thornton, at a cousin's wedding in Ballinrobe. It was love at first sight and they were married within six months – no threshing parties for them! Mike took his new bride to live at White O'Morning in Inisfree, five miles and maybe a half from Castletown, where the Thorntons had lived for seven generations. The young couple were blissfully happy as only newlyweds can be. There were no roses around White O'Morning when May came to make it her home, but she soon planted some – wild roses from the fields and a few slips of the more cultivated variety which the Vicar's wife allowed her to cut from her garden. Soon there were roses everywhere and people came from miles around to see them, they were that bright and colourful. Mike used to tease her unmercifully about them, but at the back of it all she could see that he was as proud as punch of both the roses and his lovely young wife.

Mother and child on the stepping stones over the brook in front of White O'Morn.

Before the year was out their happiness turned to even greater joy when they found they were expecting their first child. "If it is God's will", declared Mike, "it'll be a boy to help me on the farm, and we'll call him Sean after my father Sean". Old Sean Thornton, so called even though he had only just turned fifty, had been born in White O'Morning and was happy to share it with May and Mike, especially since his wife, Mike's mother, had died just a couple of years previously. He welcomed a woman's touch about the house and now there was a prospect of a grandchild. Boys oh boys!

Right enough, the baby was a boy, a strapping healthy young child and they called him Sean Thornton. He

Man and baby in front of White O'Morn.

was baptised by Father Lonergan in Saint Anselm's Church and the celebration went on well into the night. This was the young lad who now clutched his mother's hand in the laneway in front of White O'Morning, a bit mystified as to what was happening to him and why he had to leave home. He loved the countryside around Inisfree and his native fields. One of the highlights of each week was running up on a Sunday morning ahead of his parents to the little chapel along a road that wound and wound.

Sean was a well-behaved young lad, but not above getting into the odd scrape – despite his parents' warnings he could be bold and adventurous. Only a few weeks previously he had kicked his battered old football into the field where Dan Tobin's prized and feared bull was in residence. He knew he shouldn't go in to retrieve the ball, but being a fighting Thornton he did and only barely escaped with his life. The bull saw him just as he was picking up the ball – maybe it was his emerald green shirt that gave him away – and gave chase. Sean made it to the four-bar gate just in time and vaulted it in terror just inches away from the bull's horns. As he sat on the grass margin of the roadside sobbing with fear and relief, with his nose running pathetically over his geansaí, who came along but a young 'spoiled priest', Michaeleen Óg Flynn, on extended leave from the seminary. He wiped Sean's nose clean, mopped up his tears and returned him safely to his grateful parents.

It was around this time that the luck of the Thornton family took a turn for the worse. Old Sean Thornton had a strong Fenian streak in him and resented authority, especially the police and military. He enjoyed being called a 'fighting Thornton' and liked to live up to the name. He was not above taking part in raiding parties (what the authorities called 'agrarian outrages') where cattle, horses, sheep and goats were set loose, houses were burned down and crops were destroyed. These attacks were often directed at people who had occupied the houses and lands of those who had been evicted for non-payment of rent. One night, the police were tipped off about such a raid by a local informer (many suspected the tinker Nolan but nothing was ever proved) and lay in wait for the attackers. In the resulting skirmish, a peeler was shot and died a few days later from his wounds. Old Sean Thornton was arrested on suspicion of having been involved in the affair, as indeed he was, but there wasn't enough evidence to convict him of the murder – if there had been, he would have been hanged. As it was, he was convicted on a lesser charge, sentenced to penal servitude for life and transported to Australia, never to return again to Inisfree and Ireland. Eventually, news came that he had died in a penal colony in Australia – Michaeleen Óg Flynn always believed that he was hanged there after having escaped from jail in a vain attempt to return to his family in Ireland.

After his father's transportation to Australia, Mike Thornton was never the same again. He missed the old man terribly and failed to find consolation even in his lovely young wife and son. He took to drinking heavily and was to be seen every evening propping up the bar in the Sarsfield Arms, as Pat Cohan had grandly named his tavern in Inisfree. Many a time Old Sean and Mike used to have a social drink there – just one or two before returning to White O'Morning – but now Mike's drinking was no longer just a simple pleasure. He drank every night to excess and way beyond his meagre income, so much so that the family often went hungry and lacked even the basic necessities.

Then, one stormy night, the inevitable happened.

Mike Thornton was staggering home in a drunken stupor along the path by the river. At the very spot where years later his son Sean was to knock Red Will Danaher clean off the bank with a mighty punch into the water, Mike Thornton tripped over the root of a tree and fell headlong into the river. There was nobody there to give a man a hand and in his drunken condition he could do nothing to save himself. Even his ox-like shoulders were no use to him and he drowned near that very spot in just a foot and a half of water. His body was recovered a few days later from Lough Corrib. "A bad accident that", was Father Lonergan's terse comment, but behind that simple statement lay a huge tragedy for Sean and his mother and the community of Inisfree in general.

A long shot of White O'Morning taken in 1951 during the filming

May Thornton was of course devastated by her husband's tragic death – Sean was as yet too young to understand the situation fully, but he knew that life as he knew and loved it would never be the same again. May was not only emotionally shattered – she and her son were penniless and dependent on neighbours for even their food. Missus Tillane and her husband, always good to the poor, were generous and kind, but May was a proud woman and did not want herself and her son to be dependent on charity. At the earliest opportunity, she sold White O'Morning and the few acres surrounding it to the Tillane Estate for £20 – enough for the passage to America and a little more. Her brother Frank had emigrated to Pittsburgh some years previously and offered help and accommodation to May and Sean in the New World.

Now as they walked sadly down the little laneway from White O'Morning, the dawn air charged with the sweet smell of the blackcurrant bushes that lined its margins, carrying their sad little suitcases packed with their few possessions and some food for the long journey, they had little knowledge of what lay in store for them. When they crossed the brook there waiting for them was a pony and trap provided by the Tillane family, good to the poor to the last. From there they sped to Castletown Station to catch the southbound train. They steamed through stations whose names they had only just heard about – Ballyglunin, Athenry, Ennis and the great city of Limerick. After a short stop, they headed south once again, through Charleville and onto Mallow, the home of the Rakes, until finally they reached the southern capital of Cork. From there it was a short few miles to the harbour of Queenstown, where a great ocean liner was waiting for them. Neither May nor Sean had ever seen a ship so big in their lives, but during the long and rough Atlantic crossing they were both so sick, that many times they wished a tidal wave would engulf them and end it all.

After what seemed like an eternity, they arrived in New York, where Uncle Frank was waiting to greet them with a hearty welcome, but like many Irish emigrants of the time they found that America was not the paradise they expected. Times were hard and money was scarce and the only accommodation they could find was a shack near the slag heaps in the great industrial city of Pittsburgh. While

Sean went to school, May found a job in a clothing factory, working long hours on piecework for a small wage, scarcely enough to keep body and soul together. As Sean grew up and became more and more Americanised, his memories of Ireland faded, but his mother's stories never let him forget his roots and 'Inisfree' became another word for heaven for him.

Despite several proposals, May Thornton never remarried but devoted herself almost entirely to the upbringing of her son on whom she lavished all her love and affection. Soon Sean was helping out with the family income – before school every morning in true American fashion he had a paper round, and after school and at weekends he was a newsboy at Pittsburgh street corners in the searing heat of summer and the icy chill of winter, a few dollars hard-earned. Sean was only twelve when tragedy struck for a second time, just as he and his mother seemed to have turned the corner leading out of the poverty trap towards a little more comfortable life. The sweatshop May Thornton slaved in was a cramped overcrowded building designed for production and profit and certainly not for worker comfort and safety. Just a week before Christmas around the turn of the century a fire broke out, and quickly spread. There were no fire escapes or emergency exits and within minutes the building was a blazing inferno. Many lost their lives, including May Thornton, who, engulfed by the flames on the fourth storey, jumped to her death in the street below in a vain attempt to save herself. There was no insurance, compensation or social security for her sole dependent.

The house of the Widow Tillane in the grounds of Ashford Castle, now demolished.

The twelve year old Sean was naturally shattered. Here he was, an orphan in an alien country and Uncle Frank, with the best will in the world, was in no position to support him. But Sean was tough and resourceful – he left school and begged a job as a sweeper of loose material on the floors of the Pittsburgh steelworks and because of his tragic circumstances he was given one. He worked hard and gradually moved up in status to labourer, stoker and finally steel puddler. As he himself said to Michaeleen Óg Flynn, Sean grew up on steel and pig-iron furnaces so hot a man forgot his fear of hell. But there were other factors, many other experiences which shaped the young Sean Thornton: when the United States belatedly entered the Great War in Europe, Sean was quick to volunteer for the army of his adopted country. As a soldier, he sailed to Europe, thinking as he passed the Irish coast how wonderful it would be to return to his native Inisfree. His lack of money made that ambition impossible to realise at that time, and besides, there was another job to be done. He only dimly understood the fight for Irish freedom that was taking place at the same time and felt that he had a responsibility there also, but first things first.

In later life, Sean would never talk about his experiences in World War One. He saw action in the trenches and went over the top and was one of a handful of lucky survivors as many of his fellow soldiers were butchered and slaughtered about him. To survive he had to kill German soldiers in hand-to-hand combat, and the memory of this caused him flashbacks and recurrent nightmares for many years afterwards. He acquired what amounts to a split personality – he loathed fighting and killing but, on the other hand, he had to accept the fact that there were situations in which fighting involving the risk of killing was the only way out.

But the war was soon over and Sean returned to the United States. Soon the Depression was to set in and make employment difficult to find – there was no longer any place for him in the steel industry. One of his mother's fanciful stories told him of Con of the Hundred Battles and, as a fighting Thornton, what better way could he find to sublimate his aggressive tendencies than to become a prize-fighter in the noble Irish tradition of John L. Sullivan and James J. Corbett? Under the civilised rules of the great Marquis of Queensberry, the fighting would always be fair and non-fatal and besides, the money could be very good for a skilled pugilist.

Sean began modestly – fairground challenges for $10, which he won easily. Next, he sparred with experienced professionals where he learned a subtle blend of defence and attack. Finally, he became a full-time boxer. As he progressed, he improved, winning bout after bout, and becoming a formidable mixture of brawn and brain. All the time, the money rolled in and he knew that he had found his true vocation. In time he was being mentioned as a contender for the heavyweight boxing championship of the world – the top of the tree to which several Irishman had climbed previously. Finally, Sean was offered his chance – an elimination for a big purse against another heavyweight contender, Tony Gardello, with the winner to fight the current world heavyweight champion for the title.

Before we get to this crucial event in Sean Thornton's life, there is another equally important matter to be mentioned. Shortly after he returned from the war in Europe, Sean had fallen in love. The object of his affections was, fittingly enough, an American-born girl of Irish ancestry. Her name was Kathleen Thompson, an exquisitely beautiful redhead, whose parents had emigrated from the County Galway around the turn of the century. Kathleen was his soul mate, the most wonderful thing that had ever happened to him and he dreamed that one day he would take her back home to Ireland. She felt just the same way about him and within a year of meeting they were married and blissfully happy. Kathleen didn't like the fight game very much, not least because she felt it would ruin Sean's good looks, but he swore that when he was heavyweight champion and had made enough money he would quit the ring and take her back to Ireland.

Sean had, by this time, become a cult figure in the fight game. He called himself "Trooper Thorn, the fighting Irishman" and for his large following of fanatical fans, he sported a large green shamrock on his gown before each fight. The more bouts he won the larger his following became. In time, even the sports writers began to take him seriously and he became their favourite for the title.

Another tragedy was to hit Sean under the belt, and the whole thing started in the simplest and most innocent way possible. His beloved wife Kathleen was tidying out the attic of the old house they had bought and planned to make their new home, when she scratched her finger on a rusty nail covered in cobwebs. At first they thought nothing of it – just a discoloured swelling on her finger, but as the days went by it grew more painful and serious and she began to suffer the severe symptoms of blood poisoning. She was rushed to hospital but despite the best medical care she died within a few days.

Sean was once again shattered – why had Fate dealt him so many foul blows? First his grandfather, then his father and mother in turn, next his comrades in arms, and now, most cruelly of all, his beautiful and beloved wife. And just when his big chance for a tilt at the heavyweight boxing championship of the world was coming up. What should he do? One part of him said that he should end it all by his own hand and join his dead loved ones – for a time he seriously wrestled with the temptation. A tragically unwise clerical friend advised him to channel all his anger and frustration into the coming fight.

The opposing contender was Tony Gardello, a clean fighter with a nice little wife and home and a couple of kids. Sean, perhaps subconsciously jealous of his opponent's wife and family, went into the ring not to out-box him but to beat his brains out, to drive him into the canvas and to murder him. It was easy to say that he did it for a purse, a piece of the gate, lousy money, but it is more likely that Sean

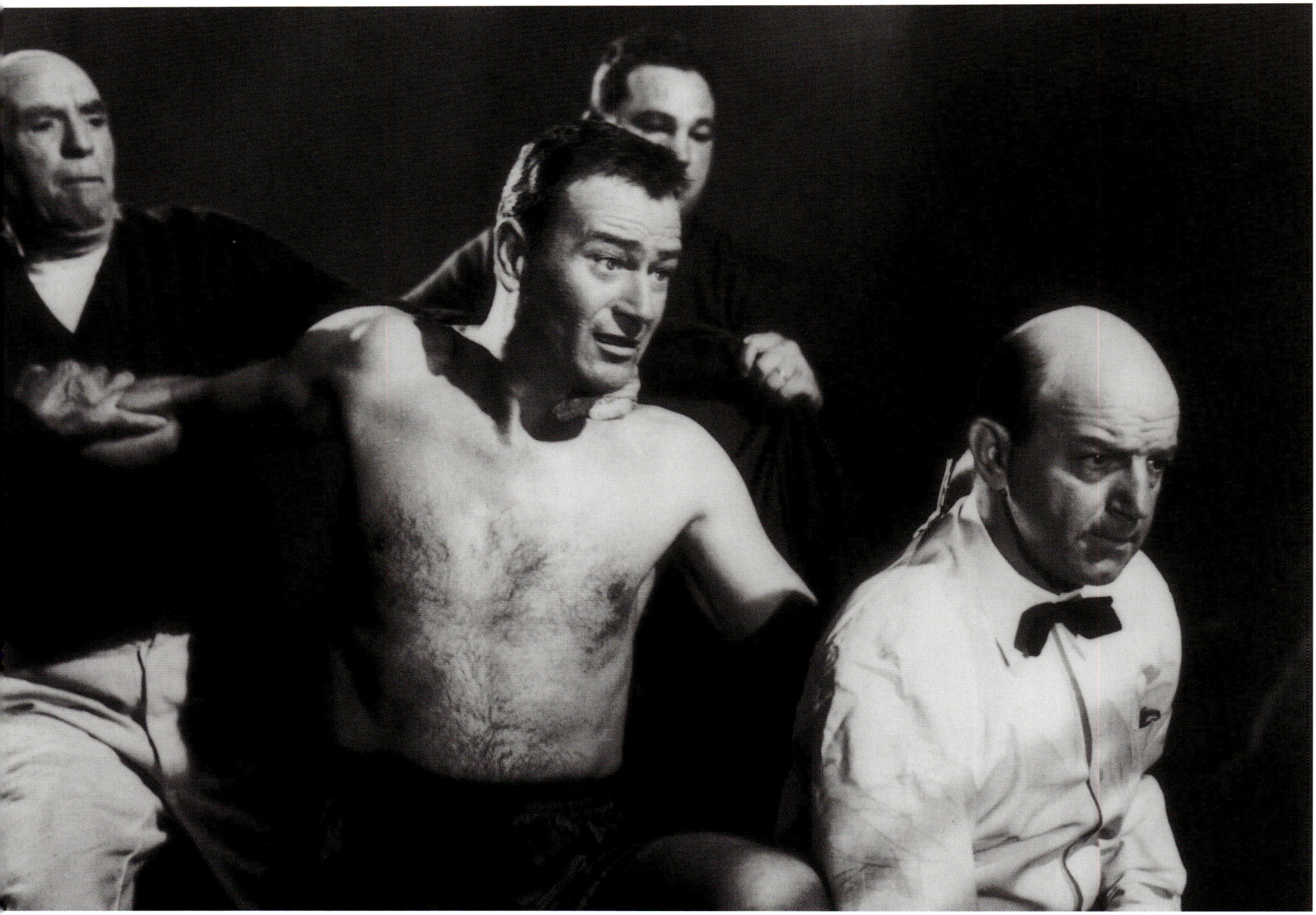

Studio still of the scene in which Trooper Thorn (John Wayne) has killed a boxer in the ring. On the left Bob Perry, centre is Tony Canzoneri and on the right is referee Al Murphy.

was hitting out like an angry child at an unseen agent that had caused him so much grief and sorrow. The moment Gardello was counted out and failed to get up, Sean realised with horror what he had done – he had murdered his opponent just as surely as if he had shot him in the head and the law couldn't and wouldn't lay a finger on him. He didn't need the doctor to enter the ring to tell him that his opponent was dead – he knew by instinct that he was and a look of horror enveloped his sweat-covered face. The world would say it was "just one of those things", but Sean knew he was responsible for the death of an innocent man and would have to live with this guilt for the rest of his days.

Where was he to turn? Although he was now a serious contender for the title he knew he could never fight again unless he was mad enough to kill and that was out of the question. So he quit the ring – just like that, without a moment's hesitation. His many fans were sorely disappointed; they understood the reasons for his decision, but secretly they hoped he would reconsider and change his mind after a decent interval had elapsed. But Sean was determined – America held too many bad memories for him. There was poverty, then the deaths of his mother and wife, and maybe worst of all, Gardello's death which was his fault and his alone. There was only one place for him to go, to that heaven on earth his mother had told him about – Inisfree and White O'Morning. Back in his Irish womb, he would be safe again, free from all risks and danger and, best of all, nobody, but nobody, would recognise him as Trooper Thorn, the killer fighter. In Inisfree he could become Sean Thornton again, son of Mike Thornton and grandson of old Sean Thornton, the Fenian hero who died in Australia. He would return to Ireland and forget the past.

At least the fight game had given him riches beyond his wildest dreams, at a huge price of course, but Sean was wise enough to realise that financial independence could help him achieve his dreams. So he sold his house and all his belongings, paid off his manager and bought a one-way ticket to Ireland. And he did something else that very few knew about – he paid a handsome sum of money to Tony Gardello's widow. That of course didn't bring her husband back but it eased the burden of widowhood and bringing up a young family alone (something he knew about himself) and Sophia Gardello was very grateful to him. She never blamed Sean for her husband's death and within a few years she had remarried.

So Sean packed his meagre luggage and set off for Ireland with a heavy heart but in some ways he was full of hope. His journey was the reverse of the childhood voyage that he scarcely remembered. This time the weather was kinder and he had a relaxing crossing in the warm spring sunshine. Disembarking from the transatlantic liner at Queenstown (now Cobh) he travelled by train via Cork and Limerick to Castletown. On his finger he still wore the gold wedding ring which he had promised Kathleen he would never take off as long as he lived.

The returned emigrant Sean Thornton (John Wayne) dressed in his Irish tweed costume.

On the last leg of the train journey from Galway to Castletown, Sean was joined in his carriage by a pleasant woman with two children, a boy and a girl. The woman's first name was Ruth (he never did find out her surname) and the children were called Freddie and Darla. The little girl snuggled her head shyly up against her mother but the little boy asked her in a whisper if he might give the

The train approaches Castletown Station bearing the returning emigrant Sean Thornton to his native land. Waiting are the Fishwoman (May Craig) and the porter (Paddy O'Donnell).

stranger an apple. When his mother gave permission, Freddie reached into a basket on the carriage floor, took out an apple and polished it on his sleeve. Then he offered it to Sean who grinned and accepted it. But he was too overcome with emotion to eat it as they neared Castletown Station so he put it in his pocket for consumption later.

Suddenly he was in Castletown and the train shuddered to a halt. On the platform there was a middle-aged porter and some men with lights and cameras – surely the press hadn't tumbled to his return already. No, just some Americans making a "movie" – a harmless activity that would be forgotten about in a few years. As he looked out the window of his carriage he saw a beautiful old lady in a shawl advancing towards the train and waving to him. His heart leapt. For a moment he thought it was his mother come to meet him and welcome him home. But no, reality intervened – his mother had died tragically in America when he was twelve and now lay in a pauper's grave. But Sean was a man now, a quiet man, and he could cope with reality.

He gathered his few pieces of luggage and stepped out onto the platform. Then he suddenly remembered his manners and held up the apple to his young benefactor saying "thanks". Over the public address system, a clerical gentleman was giving a running commentary on his arrival, a fact that struck Sean as strange, but this was Ireland. On the platform were gathered the oddest bunch of people he had ever seen – a porter, an old lady (who turned out to be a fish-woman), the guard of the train, the station master (poorly made-up and muttering "Castletown, Castletown") and soon the engine driver and the fireman of the train. Sean foolishly asked, "Can you tell me the way to Inisfree"

Returned emigrant Sean Thornton arrives at Castletown Railway Station and meets the eccentric natives. Left to right: Paddy O'Donnell, May Craig, Webb Overlander, Kevin Lawless, Joseph O'Dea and Eric Gorman.

and almost wished he hadn't. He was treated to five minutes of Irish Bulls, advice about the best place to fish and even information about the best road not to take to Inisfree. But then a little man in a black suit and wearing a bowler hat calmly took control of the situation. Without as much as a "by your leave" he took Sean's luggage and waltzed off towards the station exit door. Here he stopped and said simply

INISFREE, THIS WAY

Sean smiled and followed him with that peculiar sideways walk of his. He knew he was home at last.

His cabman was of course Michaeleen Óg Flynn – both men recognised each other at once but in that peculiar Irish fashion, both pretended not to. It would be a dramatic surprise for both of them a little later on, just to make life more interesting. As they sped towards Inisfree on Michaeleen's sidecar, they suddenly came upon the bridge over the brook, so they stopped there. As Sean looked across at "the humble cottage", his beloved White O'Morning, he felt he could hear his mother May's voice saying "Do you remember, Seanín, and how it was?" recalling all the happy moments of his childhood. He wanted to linger, but Michaeleen was worried about closing time so they travelled on. And who did they meet but Father Peter Lonergan who knew Sean's people well and had even baptised him. When Father Lonergan wanted a few private words with Michaeleen about a little matter of turf accountancy, Sean walked on ahead. Suddenly, as if in a dream, a beautiful

Sean Thornton stands on the bridge for his first close-up view of his ancestral home White O'Morn. Watching his every move is Michaeleen Óg Flynn (Barry Fitzgerald).

shepherdess stepped out from under the trees with her flock of sheep. Was she real? She couldn't be! But this time there was no doubt – it was his beautiful red-haired wife Kathleen, back from the dead to live with him in Ireland. Surely now he would be happy and there would be no more conflict. Or would there be?

Chapter Two

The True Origins of The Quiet Man

Fictional characters are more often than not based on real people of the author's acquaintance, but it is rare to find a fictional character based exclusively on a single person. That would be too obvious, too simple, and in a legal context, perhaps too dangerous. So it is too with fictional events. Fictional characters and events are more likely to be based on an amalgamation of several real-life characters and events of the author's experience, with a dash of imagination thrown in for good measure. The resulting mixture can be curiously satisfying, improving on both reality and nature, and this is perhaps one of the reasons why good fiction has had so many devoted followers over the ages.

When I wrote *The Complete Guide to the Quiet Man*, hereinafter referred to as CGQM, published in the year 2000 by Appletree Press of Belfast, I recounted faithfully the long-accepted story of Maurice Walsh's inspiration for the character of Shawn Kelvin/Paddy Bawn Enright/Sean Thornton, as the hero of *The Quiet Man* was known at various stages of his development. The Walsh family's factotum, Paddy Bawn Enright, was certainly an inspiration, right down to his exact name in one version of the story, but he was not the only inspiration.

When I was contacted in December 2001 by J.J. Bunyan of Fermoy, a native of Kerry, telling me that he had hitherto unpublished information on the inspiration for the *Quiet Man*, I admit that I was at first sceptical. Why had such exciting material not come to light before now? Where had it lain hidden for so long? However, my doubts soon vanished when J.J. Bunyan produced the documentation, most tellingly a letter in Maurice Walsh's own hand, which removed all doubt about the authenticity of the story. I am exceedingly grateful to Mr. Bunyan who has very kindly given me *carte blanche* to reproduce the material as I see fit. The story was originally told by his uncle, Thomas J. McElligott, who was born in Philadelphia in 1902. In brief the story is as follows:

Paddy Bawn Enright, one of the original inspirations for the character of Sean Thornton in The Quiet Man.

One of the original inspirations for the story of the *Quiet Man* was John McElligott of Bedford, Listowel, County Kerry, who was born in the late eighteen hundreds. He was nicknamed "Quiet Jack" by some of his neighbours because he was a very mild-mannered person. As a young man he emigrated to the United States and settled in Philadelphia, where he met and married Catherine Sheahan, who had emigrated from Glin,

The inspiration for The Quiet Man, John McElligott pictured with his wife Catherine.

County Limerick, near the Mouth of the Shannon, some time previously.

John McElligott was a superb athlete and excelled at long distance running and marathons and while in the United States he became a professional boxer. He fought and drew with both Peter Mahar and Joe Grimm in Philadelphia, boxing bare-knuckle, when a round ended only with a knock down. He was also a sparring partner of Jim Corbett who took the world heavyweight boxing title in 1892 from John L. Sullivan, another boxer of North Kerry ancestry. Interestingly, Corbett in turn lost his title in 1897 to the inventor of the solar plexus punch, Bob Fitzsimmons, who shared his surname with Maureen O'Hara.

Catherine and John McElligott's son Thomas was born in 1902 and a few years afterwards, the family returned to Ireland. Thomas recalls an incident that took place around 1914 when he and his father John took some cattle to sell at Listowel fair. There was a big cattle "jobber" from Dublin there buying cattle freely – he stood six foot four to John McElligott's five foot eleven inches. The big jobber liked the look of McElligott's cattle and agreed to buy them. The parties shook hands and no doubt spat on hands too to seal the bargain.

Now in the Ireland of the day there was a lovely custom called the "luck penny" which still survives in some rural pockets. After cattle were paid for at the fair it was customary to return a small amount of the money to the buyer so that the cattle would have "luck" with them i.e. that they would be healthy and not suffer from any serious disease. There is more than a hint here that the luck penny was an offering to appease evil spirits or even the "little people". Well, when the big Dublin cattle jobber paid for the McElligott's cattle he deducted the luck penny from the price he handed over, without waiting to have it returned to him as was customary.

"Wait a minute", said John McElligott, no doubt quietly. "Pay me what we agreed upon, and let my generosity determine the luck penny".

"Listen Jack", said the jobber. "Take what you got and go home, before I flatten you here in the market place".

John McElligott put all of the money in the jobber's hand and said "I'll give you back all the money if you can flatten me here in the market place, but if I flatten you, you'll have to pay me double".

"Done", said the jobber *à la* Michaeleen Óg Flynn, and like the railway crew they took their coats off as the inevitable crowd gathered round. At this stage young Thomas began to cry loudly because he was afraid his father was going to be killed, but, like Danaher, the jobber was blissfully ignorant that he was swapping punches with a professional boxer who had sparred with the heavyweight champion of the world. John McElligott landed a hard right on the jobber's jaw and he went down only to claim that he had fallen because the ground was wet and slippery. (Well, give a man a hand then!) Up he jumped and they swapped punches, but soon the jobber was on his back again. This time he conceded and agreed to pay double the agreed price for the cattle. (You've had enough? Here's your dirty money).

However, after he was paid, John (Sean) generous-

Top: John McElligott, the all-round athlete.
Bottom: John McElligott of Listowel Co. Kerry in boxing pose in the USA. He is now believed to be the main inspiration for the Quiet Man, the character first conceived by Kerry author Maurice Walsh.

ly announced to the thirsty onlookers "Drinks for everyone" and they all marched off to the nearest pub. That evening he arrived home to his wife Catherine (Kate) probably inebriated and without a penny to show for his day's work. All of this true story bears an uncanny resemblance to *The Quiet Man*, and thus it appears that the unpaid luck penny eventually became an unpaid dowry – he's sold the crossbreds, he can't say he hasn't got the money with him now.

In 1956, a grandson of John McElligott, Eddie McElligott, then a Carmelite priest, Father Kenneth, in Rome, was taking a course in English literature, and was so struck by the resemblance of the plot of *The Quiet Man* to the family story he had so often heard, that he later decided to write to Maurice Walsh to inquire if there was any connection. Walsh graciously conceded the source of his inspiration and even more – he confessed that he was a blood relation of the McElligotts! Here is the letter in full:

Green Rushes, Avoca Road, Blackrock, Co. Dublin.
9 June 1960.
Dear Fra. Kenneth,

Got your letter of the 4th inst. I think you and I are related by blood. My father (God rest him) was John Walsh of Ballydonoghue – now a parish in its own right – and my brother Paddy still has the old farm. I don't quite remember your grandfather but I heard of him. I left home in 1900 to enter the Excise Service. Our relation, I think, is through the O'Connors of Tullamore and the McElligotts of Gunsboro. I'll make some inquiries next time I am down.

I used two incidents in that story of the *Quiet Man*: one where the bully refused to pay his sister's fortune at Listowel Fair and the *Quiet Man* did nothing; the other where your grandfather showed up a cheat before the whole market. I combined the two incidents, made some changes, and sold the story to the S[aturday] E[vening] Post and to John Ford who made a film of it. I'm glad you traced my inspiration.

If (D.V.) I am in the land of the living next year I shall hope to meet you here in Ireland.

God bless you in your vocation,
Yours Aye,
Maurice Walsh

Incidentally, Thomas McElligott, who related the incident of the fight at the fair, later saw active service on the Republican side in the Civil War in Ireland during the period 1922-23. This provides yet another link with the original *Quiet Man* story as told in *Green Rushes*.

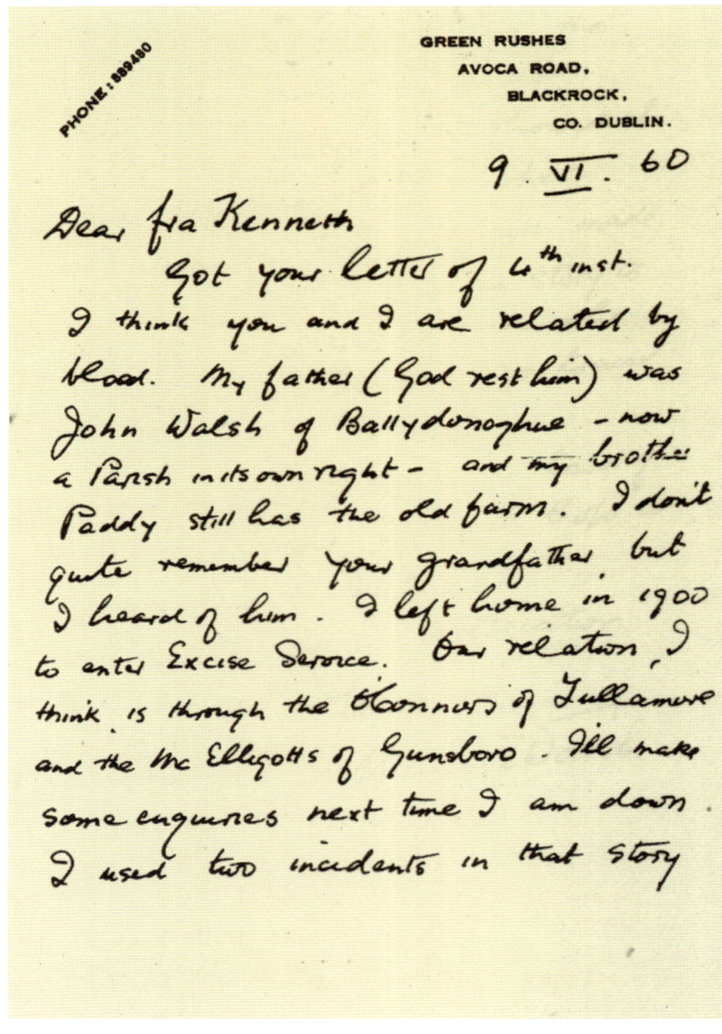

PHONE: 889480
GREEN RUSHES
AVOCA ROAD,
BLACKROCK,
CO. DUBLIN.

9. VI. 60

Dear Fra Kenneth
Got your letter of 4th inst.
I think you and I are related by blood. My father (God rest him) was John Walsh of Ballydonoghue - now a Parish in its own right - and my brother Paddy still has the old farm. I don't quite remember your grandfather but I heard of him. I left home in 1900 to enter Excise Service. Our relation, I think, is through the O'Connors of Tullamore and the McElligotts of Gunsboro. I'll make some enquiries next time I am down. I used two incidents in that story

Copy of letter sent from Maurice Walsh to Father Kenneth McElligott.

Chapter Three

The Quiet Man Train and the Playfair Car

Several of John Ford's movies begin with the time-honoured device of a train pulling into a station. In *The Man Who Shot Liberty Valance* (1962) the train represents the gap between the past and the present, giving an excuse for very effective flashback scenes and helping to make this one of Ford's most powerful productions. The middle segment of *The Rising of the Moon* (1957) has a more prosaic motivation for using a train – the entire action of this comic third of the movie takes place in a railway station. But in *The Quiet Man*, the train and the railway station of Ballyglunin (Castletown) assume a much wider significance, giving the movie a solid steel and brick core as it were, and becoming an essential part of the plot and the action. When Sean Thornton steps off the train, he is stepping backwards in time out of the New World and into the old Irish West, even to the extent of a real horse replacing an iron horse. Later on in the movie when Mary Kate's attempts her (mock?) escape from the husband she thinks is a coward, in an echo of the opening scene, Sean quickly arrives on a grass and oats powered engine and denies the steam engine of its lovely cargo.

But what of the *Quiet Man* train itself? As well as being a gigantic movie prop, it was of course a real engine, in regular service on the Tuam-Athenry-Galway line (opened in 1894) and rented by Ford, complete with railway crew. Irish railway buffs (to whom I am greatly indebted for information) knew it simply as No. 59 and its brightly coloured number is one of the very first things we see in the movie as the train puffs proudly into Castletown station bearing the hero of *The Quiet Man*.

No. 59 was one of a group of ten very similar steam locomotives built between 1883 and 1890 by the Great Southern and Western Railway Company (later Coras Iompar Eireann (CIE) and later still Iarnród Eireann or Irish Rail). Technically, No. 59 was a McDonnell-designed D17 4.4.0 engine, built at the Inchicore works in Dublin in 1888 under the aegis of locomotive superintendent J.A.F. Aspinall. It carried a saturated 52-class boiler and was fitted with an outside 1864 gallon tender. Like its sisters, No. 59 was a passenger locomotive as distinct from the many goods locomotives on the line, and the group was unique in being the first "bogie" locomotives of the G.S.W.R. with wheel arrangement 4-4-0. Six-wheel rolling stock was also used, notably in *The Quiet Man*, and the original G.S.W.R. livery was olive-green with black and red lines. In 1974, railway historian Drew Donaldson wrote:

> In postwar years No. 59 was giving a good account of herself on the Tuam-Galway line (mostly working the 3pm to Galway). On one occasion in 1952, engine driver Paddy Ryan got her up to as much as 64 miles per hour on the Ballyglunin-Athenry section of the track. As well as being a film star, 59 (a beautifully steady engine) was a great "pet" at Athenry shed, which struggled on with a leaky foundation ring, afraid to send their inamorata to Inchicore in case she might never return.

Ballyglunin closed to scheduled passenger services on July 10th 1967 but the cabin and loop were used for trains carrying sugar beet for the Tuam factory until 1980 after which it did not reopen. For some time in the 1990s a special train for *Quiet Man* fans ran on the line but it was discontinued after a fire on board. But, even as I write, in the West on Track Committee, have an ongoing campaign to secure the reopening of the Western Rail Corridor from Galway to Sligo. During one of their events they re-

A view of the filming at Castletown Station (Ballyglunin) taken from a camera on the railway bridge.

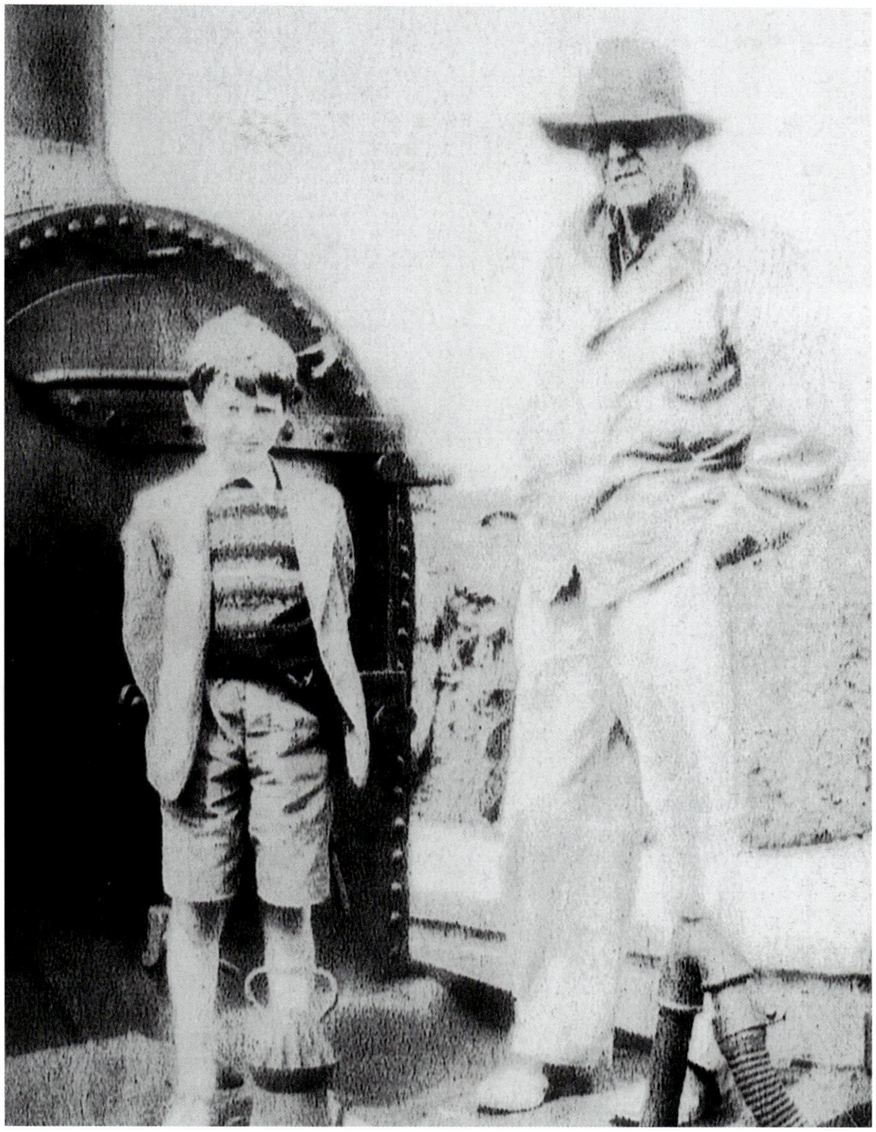

Right: Young Cormac O'Malley, son of Ernie O'Malley, poses with John Ford on top of Engine No. 59.
Left: Mary Kate Danaher (Maureen O'Hara) poses with Cormac O'Malley and the train crew at Ballyglunin.

enacted scenes from *The Quiet Man* shot in Ballyglunin to get publicity for their cause and the many fans of the movie worldwide will undoubtedly wish them success.

The footbridge at Ballyglunin, as we have related in CGQM, now proudly does service at Ballinasloe Station in East Galway. However, Ballyglunin was not its first home. The footbridge was built by Ross and Walpole in Dublin in 1891, and it was assigned to Oughterard station in Connemara on the Galway-Clifden line, first opened in 1895. This of course was the very line on which Ford first planned to shoot *The Quiet Man*, being the nearest railway track to his beloved Galway homestead in Spiddal, but the filming was delayed for so long that by the time in 1951 that the finances, cast and crew were all in place, the line had long since closed (April 27th 1935). However, wittingly or unwittingly, the canny Ford had managed to include prominently in *The Quiet Man* a relic of his originally intended location in full colour!

The Quiet Man train, No. 59 stands in Tuam Station

And what of the gallant engine No. 59? Like most of her sisters, she kept going right up to the end of the steam era and she was scrapped, smelted, or recycled, call it what you will, in 1959. What a pity she was not preserved as a museum piece, preferably in Ballyglunin or Cong – what a tourist attraction that would have been! As my good friend and informant Sean Teegan has remarked, a lifetime of over seventy years faithful service on the track speaks volumes for her designers, builders and operating staff. And who knows, maybe its recycled steel is still doing a good job somewhere.

But the truth is that No. 59 will roll forever, or at least as long as *The Quiet Man* is being viewed on video, DVD or in the cinema. Statisticians estimate that at any given moment in time, somebody, and probably several people, on this planet are viewing *The Quiet Man* and watching that train roll into Castletown to begin the greatest adventure in movie history. And Spielberg's ET was clearly so captivated that he took a copy with him when he returned home, so engine No. 59 is rolling perpetually, not just on this earth, but in far-flung corners of the Universe.

Top: The tracks at Ballyglunin Station (Castletown) along which Sean Thornton (John Wayne) rode his horse to snatch his new bride Mary Kate (Maureen O'Hara) from the Dublin train.

Top right: The Railway Porter, local man Paddy O'Donnell, poses on the sundial at Ashford Castle.

Centre left: The window at Ballyglunin Station through which Sean Thornton saw the jaunting car for the first time.

Centre right: The railway bridge that featured in The Quiet Man It is shown as it stands today in the station at Ballinasloe in East Galway.

Bottom: Re-enactment of The Quiet Man drag scene at Ballyglunin Railway Station in 2003 as part of the 'Save the Western Railway" Campaign.

Top: John Ford clowns about with extras and bit part players in Cong as Mr. Playfair (Arthur Shields) drives the Bishop (Philip Stainton) through Inisfree.
Bottom left: Playfair's Morris Cowley car takes a well-earned break in Ashford Grounds. Included in the picture are Lord Killanin, Charles Fitzsimons and Paddy O'Donnell.
Bottom right: Rev. Cyril Playfair (Arthur Shields) arrives in style with the Bishop (Philip Stainton).

Sean Thornton (John Wayne) pays his respects to the Bishop (Philip Stainton) and Rev. Cyril Playfair as he drags Mary Kate (Maureen O'Hara) past Ashford Castle.

The Bishop (Philip Stainton) rides in state through Inisfree in IM2234.

Maureen O'Hara and Family

The lovely Maureen O'Hara arrives in Ireland

Left: Maureen O'Hara waits to go on camera in Cong on the set of The Quiet Man.

Below: Maureen O'Hara on location in the grounds of Ashford Castle. The coat is to keep out the chill of the Irish summer!

Above: Maureen O'Hara takes some time out at Ashford Castle to read Richard Hayward's 'The Corrib Country'.
Above Right: Maureen O'Hara rehearses the song 'The Isle of Innisfree' with Danny Borzage of the Sons of the Pioneers on set in the Hollywood studios.
Bottom Left: The beautiful young Maureen O'Hara pictured with her mother while visiting relatives in Castlebar, County Mayo.
Bottom Right: Maureen O'Hara pictured with her lovely daughter, Bronwyn Bridgid Fitzsimons.

Below: Maureen O'Hara stands by the door of White O'Morn with members of the Joyce family.
Right: Mary Kate Danaher (Maureen O'Hara) rehearses by the ox-eye daisy wall on Ashford farm.
Below right: Mary Kate Danaher (Maureen O'Hara) waits with a bunch of flowers for Sean Thornton after the Lettergesh Races in a scene which did not appear in the final cut.

Chapter Four

Richard Farrelly and The Isle of Innisfree

Music is a vital but often neglected aspect of any motion picture. Few, if any, films attempt to dispense with it altogether, but the paradox is that it must not be intrusive – it must not be noticed, and it must certainly not detract from the visual action which is the essence of the medium. Thus film music is akin to the seasoning on food – one certainly notices if it is missing, but one tends to take it for granted when it is present.

The musical score of John Ford's *Quiet Man* has not received a great deal of attention or analysis, yet it is a vital ingredient of the movie. To see this, try watching it, as I have done, with the sound turned off – it is flat and insipid, like champagne without the bubbles. Music in *The Quiet Man* frequently determines the mood, from the clicketty-clack rhythm of *The Rakes of Mallow* which ushers in Sean Thornton on the train to Castletown, right through to the march-like *Saint Patrick's Day* with which the movie ends so joyfully.

One piece of music, however, stands head and shoulders above all of the others with which Ford chose to ornament his masterpiece, and that is Richard Farrelly's *The Isle of Innisfree* (spelled slightly differently from the village of Inisfree). The word "Innisfree" (= island of heather) was clearly inspired by the famous poem by W.B. Yeats, *The Lake Isle of Innisfree* written in 1893; but while Yeats' Innisfree was merely an uninhabited island in Sligo's Lough Gill, Farrelly's Innisfree represented all of Ireland as seen through the nostalgic eyes of an Irish emigrant. Both the music and the lyrics of the song are perfectly in keeping with the theme of *The Quiet Man* and John Ford milked it for all it was worth. Sadly, however, Ford did not see fit to include Farrelly's poignant words expressing the longing of an Irish emigrant for his native land, but, with the help of Maureen O'Hara and Charlie Fitzsimons,

The handsome features of Richard Farrelly, the policeman who composed The Isle of Innisfree, the lovely theme music of The Quiet Man.

Richard Farrelly and his lovely wife Anne in 1956 around the time of their marriage.

quickly cobbled together a single verse which was then sung by Maureen, rather beautifully one must admit, to the air of *The Isle of Innisfree* in the movie. Farrelly's lyrics one feels might have been a great deal more effective.

The melody of *The Isle of Innisfree*, however, almost totally dominates *The Quiet Man*, being reprised at least eleven times, twice in full. Whenever the emotion intensifies, whenever there is extreme passion or feeling, this memorable melody is introduced to signal that fact. With wonderful orchestration and variation, Vic Young's arrangements draw every ounce of richness from the lush melody on a variety of instruments.

We first hear it over the credits with Ashford Castle at sunset in the background; next it is played on the harp at Leam Bridge during the voice-over of Sean's mother. Naturally it is used for the glorious scene where Sean first sees Mary Kate driving sheep – was there ever in the history of the cinema a happier marriage of sight and sound? Next we hear *The*

Isle of Innisfree as the couple kiss in the cottage and Mary Kate falls in the storm as she splashes across the brook. Then it is played as Sean and Michaeleen arrive for the unsuccessful matchmaking encounter and also when Sean leaves in disgust and Mary Kate cries at the window – scenes of high emotion all. Naturally it is used to enhance the intensity of the storm scene in the graveyard; however, from then on it is used sparingly – Mary Kate sings her version and we hear it fleetingly in the rose garden and as a prelude to what we feel is the consummation of the Thornton marriage – but then we hear it no more. *The Isle of Innisfree* vanishes for the last third of *The Quiet Man* to be replaced by the more frenetic *Rakes of Mallow* which is more suited to the fighting and slapstick action. Of course at this stage it has achieved its function and the recessional Saint Patrick's Day is much more in keeping with the film's happy ending. Sadly, the composer of *The Isle of Innisfree*, Richard Farrelly, received no mention in the screen credits. So many myths and half-truths have accumulated around Farrelly and his famous song that it is perhaps now time to dispel them, and fill in the background to this remarkable man's life.

Richard Farrelly, known to his friends as Dick, was born in Kells, County Meath, in 1916, a turbulent year in Irish history. His parents were publicans who ran a bar in Church Street, Kells. When he was twenty-three, Richard left Kells for Dublin to join the Irish Police force, the Garda Siochana (literally "guardians of the peace"). He served in various Garda stations in Ireland throughout his thirty-eight year police career, ending up in the Carriage Office in Dublin Castle, formerly the centre of British rule in Ireland.

Great songwriter Richard Farrelly meets the world's greatest crooner Bing Crosby in Dublin in later life. In the centre is George O'Reilly of the Bing Crosby Society who brought them together

The signed photograph Bing Crosby presented to Richard Farrelly. The caption reads "To Dick Farrelly - Thanks for a lovely song. Bing Crosby"

By all accounts Richard Farrelly was a gentle and quiet man, a good husband to his beautiful wife Anne (Lowry) and a loving father to his three daughters and two sons. Coincidentally, his wife Anne came from Headford near where *The Quiet Man* was filmed, knew Joe Fair who doubled for Duke Wayne in the riding scenes and was actually present at the shooting of the movie in Cong, long before she met her husband.

But Richard Farrelly had a secret talent far removed from his everyday job – he was a songwriter and poet. During his lifetime he wrote over two hundred songs and poems and many of those came to light only after his death. He was a very private, modest and shy man and rarely sought publicity for his musical creations – he seems to have written and composed more for his own satisfaction than for commercial reasons. Nevertheless, before *Innisfree*, in 1948 he wrote the words and music of *If I Ever Fall in Love Again* which was a British hit for Anne Shelton and a hit for Guy Lombardo in the United States.

Early in 1949 Dick Farrelly was returning to duty in Dublin by bus from his native Kells where he had spent the weekend with his parents. Every time he left home, even though it was only a short distance away, perhaps he felt a little of the wrench that every emigrant feels – it has been said of the Irish that they can feel homesick even when they are at home! As the rural fields of Meath were gradually replaced by the concrete streets of suburban Dublin, a few scattered notes and words on the theme of how all Irish emigrants long for their rural homeland passed idly through his mind. Words and notes tumbled into place and by the time he reached Dublin the lyrics and music were almost complete and, before he went to bed that night, *The Isle of Innisfree* was safely down on paper. A bus journey of less than an hour had spawned a musical masterpiece.

Richard Farrelly's *The Isle of Innisfree* is a sumptuously beautiful song with a haunting melody of which one never tires. It is totally original and only Irish begrudgery (for which we are justly famous) could have given rise to the many false rumours about its origins. It is definitely not based on an "old Irish folk melody" (which one?). Nor is it an imitation of *Dream of Olwen* by Charles Williams from the Edward Dryhurst film *While I Live* (1947). I, and others who have musical qualifications, have listened to *Dream of Olwen* many times and can find no similarity or connection between this song and *The Isle of Innisfree*. We are at a loss to know where this fanciful story first came from and have no difficulty in dismissing it out of hand.

The Isle of Innisfree was an immediate smash hit, climbing to number two in the British Top Twenty, as the charts were then known. Dublin band leaders voted it their number one tune of the year and it was whistled and hummed by just about everyone. International fame was just around the corner – Bing Crosby recorded it in 1952 and it was one of his biggest hits in the UK. The icing on the cake was when John Ford heard it and loved it so much that he decided to use it as the principal musical theme of *The Quiet Man*. But even without these huge boosts it is interesting to note that it sold over 150,000 copies in sheet music format in the British Isles alone.

In more recent times *The Isle of Innisfree* had a huge revival when Steven Spielberg included it in *ET* (1982) during the sequence in which the little alien fools about with the makeshift TV control. It also made an appearance in the film *Distant Voices Still Lives* (1998). It has been recorded by literally hundreds of vocalists worldwide since Bing Crosby – most notably Connie Foley, Val Doonican, Joseph Locke, John McNally, Sean Dunphy, Joe Loss, Tommy Fleming, Brian Kennedy and Victor Sylvester, to mention but a few. Richard Farrelly never quite hit the same heights again as he did with *The Isle of Innisfree* – who could? – but he did continue to write songs, many with an Irish theme. His *Cottage by the Lee* is a lovely ballad, popularised by Joe Lynch, and other titles include *Rose of Slievenamon*, *There's Only One Killarney* and *We Dreamed Our Dreams*, recorded by the Furey Brothers and Davey Arthur.

Richard Farrelly died in 1990 aged 74, deeply mourned by his family and friends and music lovers everywhere. After his death, his musician son Gerard discovered an old suitcase, a treasure trove containing over two hundred poems and songs that he had written and not published during his lifetime. Many of these were in the Irish language. Gerard and his wife, the singer Sinead Stone, have put together a selection of these on a highly recommended CD entitled *Legacy Of a Quiet Man* – including *Annaghdown*, *People Like You and Me*, and of course, *The Isle of Innisfree*. Another son, Richard M. Farrelly, also features on this CD. (Details may be found on the website www.stoneandfarrelly.com).

In the early days of the cinema, film music played in the theatre or movie house on the organ or the piano merely made up for the lack of sound on the screen; it was only later, in the era of talkies, that film music assumed an importance in its own right. The specific task of composing film music came to be seen as one of the essential ingredients of any major production.

The most successful and prolific composer of all time in the field of film music is John Williams, born in Long Island, New York in 1930. Winner of five Oscars and nominated an incredible forty-one times, Williams' achievements include *Jaws* (1975); *Close Encounters of the Third Kind* (1977); *Star Wars* (1977); *Superman* (1978); *Raiders of the Lost Ark* (1981); *ET* (1982); *Jurassic Park* (1993); *Harry Potter and the Philosopher's Stone* (2001) and *Minority Report* (2002). His musical scores are not just perfectly judged movie themes, but have all become part of public consciousness and recognition in a way that has not been achieved by any other film composer. Williams has of course been closely associated with a great *Quiet Man* fan Steven Spielberg, but recently he revealed his own indebtedness to the musical judgement of John Ford.

When he was very much younger, Williams saw *The Quiet Man* in 1952 shortly after its release. He described it as a hugely romantic but quite comic film and it quickly became one of his favourite movies. At the time he was working with various orchestras in California and had no interest in film music, being chiefly concerned with playing the piano. The score arranged by Vic Young, much of it based on Irish folk melodies, turned John Williams on to the ideas of writing music for the movies. In particular, he singles out Young's arrangement of *The Rakes of Mallow* (also used by Spielberg in the movie *1941*) and the passionate and romantic *Isle of Innisfree* by Richard Farrelly as major inspiration for his own hugely successful career.

Richard Farrelly's son Gerard and his wife Sinead Stone carry on the family tradition today. They are two of Ireland's most popular recording artists.

Williams points out that in the old studio days the composer would have been given only a 10-week contract, during which time all the music would have to be written and recorded. Nowadays, the period would be more likely to be three months, because films are longer and contain more music – yet *The Quiet Man* lasted over two hours and was choc-a-bloc with music. John Williams concludes his tribute to *The Quiet Man* in the following glowing terms:

> The composer will usually study the film with the director, and discuss where in the film the music will play. Then it is a matter of analysing each scene separately and looking at details such as tempo, texture and timbre. The co-ordination of music and action is a consideration, as is the emotive impact of melodic structure. Instrumental sources are important too, and are chosen not just for texture and timbre, but also whether they relate to the period of the film, the location and the cultural background. I think that Young's music for *The Quiet Man* deals with all these elements beautifully. It is also a wonderfully well-written film, and the staging of it is expert.

This is high praise indeed from the greatest composer of film music the world has ever known and John Ford, Vic Young and Richard Farrelly can all share credit for launching the career of the great John Williams.

And finally, what of *The Isle of Innisfree* itself? It is one of the finest and most beautiful melodies ever written, ranking in the opinion of many, right beside *Danny Boy* (*The (London)Derry Air*) and no greater praise is possible. But its appeal is also timeless and international, expressing as it does the trauma of separation from one's birthplace and the ecstasy of returning to the physical soil from which one is sprung. On another level *The Isle of Innisfree* is fairy music from an enchanted world transporting Sean Thornton and the rest of us into another dimension where strange phenomena occur – beautiful barefoot red-haired ladies appear from nowhere and vanish again; impish leprechauns break through the mirage to lead us to the water of life; mysterious womb-like cottages dredged from childhood memories manifest themselves through the night mists – it's magic music, I tell you, and no wonder it has been bewitching moviegoers for over fifty years.

But it is the sheer unanswerable beauty of the melody of Richard Farrelly's *The Isle of Innisfree* that makes the greatest impact and dwells so deeply in the memory. Here is music dripping with emotion, lush texture, brimming with nostalgia, and fitting so perfectly into the action of *The Quiet Man* that it could have been written with the movie in mind. No wonder John Ford jumped on it and named the village of Inisfree in its honour – Ford knew a thing or two about choosing music for a film as he showed in *How Green Was My Valley* (1941) when he picked the most exquisite Welsh tunes. *The Quiet Man* would not have been half the film it is without the music of *The Isle of Innisfree* and we can only kneel in wonder at this result of the collaboration of three geniuses each in his own field – Victor Young, John Ford and Richard Farrelly.

Anne and Richard Farrelly in 1960 as his fame spread worldwide.

Chapter Five

Ernie O'Malley and the Quiet Man Republican Connection

John Ford was always a strong supporter of the Irish Republican movement and its struggle to win independence for Ireland. In fact, he liked to give the impression that he was personally involved in the War of Independence, but as usual it is difficult to distinguish Fordean fantasy from fact. His claim, for example, that he was present in Dublin's Shelbourne Hotel when British officers were assassinated there cannot possibly be true, because it happened in 1920, the year before Ford arrived in Ireland; on the other hand, and rather incredibly, painstaking research by Joseph McBride has revealed that Ford was actually a passenger on the *Cambria* when it sailed from Holyhead to Ireland bearing Michael Collins returning home from the treaty negotiations in London in December 1921.

However, there is no doubt that some of Ford's many Irish cousins, and in particular Martin Feeney of Spiddal, were actively involved in the Irish War of Independence and indeed were "on the run". But doubt again emerges as to whether Ford arrived in Connemara at the very moment that the family ancestral home had been torched by the Black and Tans, an incident echoed in several of his films, including *Drums Along the Mohawk*, *Liberty Valance* and *The Searchers*. Ford may very well have contributed funds to the Republican Movement in later years and as we have seen in CGQM, while in Ireland in 1951 he took part in a concert in Galway for the support of relatives of republican prisoners.

The original story by Maurice Walsh and the subsequent screenplay for *The Quiet Man* movie had a very strong IRA theme, but as various versions and rewrites emerged, this component became less and less until finally it vanished almost entirely except for a few sanitised references. Nevertheless, and probably because the aptly named Republic Pictures Corporation were footing the bill, Ford contacted the legendary IRA hero, Ernie O'Malley and offered him a job as assistant on *The Quiet Man* with the impressive title of "IRA Consultant". Ernie O'Malley was one of the most remarkable men that Ireland has produced in any age and it is impossible to do justice to his colourful and incident-packed life in a few short paragraphs (Richard English's biography *Ernie O'Malley IRA Intellectual*, Oxford University Press, 1998 is very strongly recommended).

Ernie O'Malley (1897-1957), revolutionary, writer and Renaissance man, was born in Castlebar, Co. Mayo, one of eleven children. He grew to love the rugged scenery of the West

Ernie O'Malley poses smilingly with his son Cormac at Ballyglunin Station. Note Cormac's lethal knife - this is not a family to mess with!

Three remarkable Republicans; on the left is Tom Maguire TD, Member of the Dail (Irish Parliament) and father of Bill Maguire who doubled for John Wayne in The Quiet Man; in the centre is John Ford, would-be Republican indebted to Republic Pictures; on the right is Ernie O'Malley, freedom fighter, hired by Ford as "IRA Consultant" for The Quiet Man.

of Ireland and even when his family moved to Dublin in 1906 he stayed in contact with his rural roots. He was educated by the Irish Christian Brothers at the O'Connell School, from which he proceeded to University College Dublin in 1915 to study medicine. However, his studies were interrupted by the Easter Rising of 1916, when he suddenly discovered strong nationalistic leanings, quite contrary to his family tradition. He backed the Rising enthusiastically and took an active if minor part as a rooftop sniper, although he was only eighteen at the time. After the Rebellion, he joined the Volunteers which in 1919 became the Irish Republican Army; as part of his new persona he embraced all aspects of Irish National culture – music, language, poetry, history and painting. In 1918 he abandoned his medical studies to become a full-time soldier and took a very active part in the Anglo-Irish War of Independence as a revolutionary on the run all over Ireland. He organised ambushes on British Crown forces and daring attacks on Police Barracks and almost single-handedly invented techniques of guerrilla warfare, much imitated throughout the world in the twentieth century. He was captured, tortured and imprisoned by the British authorities. True to form, he escaped from Kilmainham Jail, Dublin in February 1921.

When the Anglo-Irish Treaty was signed later in 1921, O'Malley opposed it as a dangerous compromise, since it included only twenty-six counties and involved taking an oath to a foreign king. Consequently, he became a major figure in the Irish Civil War on the Republican or Anti-Treaty side. In November 1922 he was shot and badly wounded before being arrested and imprisoned. Ironically, only the seriousness of his condition saved him from court martial and probable execution. Despite his two years in prison, he stood as a Republican candidate for the Dáil (Irish Parliament) and was duly elected for the Dublin City North Constituency. However, he never took his seat because this would have entailed taking an oath of allegiance to the British Crown. He joined in the hunger strike by Republican prisoners, holding out for forty-one days until the strike was called off. Military hostilities came to a sudden end in Spring 1923 but Ernie O'Malley was one of the last Republican prisoners to be released in July 1924. His exciting and rather incredible military and revolutionary adventures are recounted in three books he wrote – *On Another Man's Wound* (1936), *The Singing Flame* (printed 1978) and *Raids and Rallies* (printed 1982) in which accounts of the most savage and brutal military action are intermingled with breathtakingly beautiful descriptions of Nature and the Irish countryside.

In later life, Ernie O'Malley became increasingly interested and active in the arts – literature, poetry, theatre, painting and sculpture – and travelled extensively in the United States and on the continent of Europe. Among his friends and acquaintances he numbered poet Louis MacNeice, novelist Liam O'Flaherty (who had written *The Informer*, the basis of Ford's Oscar winning movie), playwright Samuel Beckett, short story writers Seán O'Faoláin and Frank O'Connor, and many other major Irish figures in the Arts. Tall, handsome, romantic and intellectual, O'Malley represented a totally different face of Irish Republicanism from those who saw it as a merely political and military struggle. He wrote about Irish artists Jack B. Yeats and Louis Le Brocquy, and

Ernie O'Malley poses at Ballyglunin Station with his son Cormac and Maureen O'Hara

was book editor for the literary magazine the *Bell* in 1947. He wrote and lectured on Mexican art for the BBC and spoke about oriental music on Radio Éireann – truly a man of amazing artistic versatility. Later, as a very real contribution to Irish historical records, he spent eight years interviewing over four hundred and fifty survivors of the War of Independence and documenting their experiences as if he were a one-man military history bureau. Sadly, despite being given a state funeral with full military honours attended by the President of Ireland, Sean T. O'Kelly and Taoiseach Eamon De Valera, when he died in 1957, O'Malley never achieved the recognition he deserved during his lifetime, and it is only now, almost fifty years after his death, that his immense contribution to Irish nationhood is at last being recognised.

Ernie O'Malley fitted perfectly into Ford's vision of the heroic Irish revolutionary, so it is no surprise that he became part of the *Quiet Man* production team. However, his duties on location turned out to be rather mundane. He was on the set every day giving Ford advice on local culture, accents and authenticity of character. One newspaper account of the time reports John Ford roaring through a megaphone for Ernie O'Malley to bring on the extras and he certainly assisted Ford in the direction of some of the crowd scenes. However, his real function seems to have been to befriend the director and reassure him that what he was portraying was acceptable in cultural and political terms. Maureen O'Hara, with whom O'Malley got on well, relates that Ford had great respect for Ernie and they would natter away on the set like old buddies – they liked each other and were good friends. One of their favourite topics of conversation was military history, particularly naval warfare. O'Malley seems to have enjoyed the film experience and no doubt the money he received came in useful too – possibly the only money he ever received from a Republican source! One of Ernie's assignments was to take John Wayne out drinking the night before the big fight in *The Quiet Man*. Generally, Ford did not approve of drinking

Irish Republican and Renaissance man Ernie O'Malley, pictured with his friend John Wayne and his admiring son Cormac O'Malley.

Ernie O'Malley, Lord Killanin and John Ford together again for the shooting of Rising of the Moon (1957). O'Malley is now credited in the titles as Earnán O'Maille, Technical Advisor

during filming, but the same story is told of using this technique on Victor McLaglen in *The Informer* and its subsequent success.

Perhaps at times O'Malley cringed at the contrast between the comic and romantic portrayal of Ireland in *The Quiet Man* and the brutal political and military bloodbath that he had been through, but doubtless he kept his feelings to himself. Perhaps Ford wanted him to appear on screen as an extra, but there is no record that he did, though as we have recounted in CGQM, his son Cormac was filmed driving a cart containing Sean chasing Mary Kate across the sand dunes of Lettergesh after the horse race, a scene that sadly did not make it to the final cut.

Interestingly, Ernie O'Malley was not carried away by Ford's reputation and kept his feet on the ground throughout their contact. He remarked that although he liked Ford, he found him difficult to work with and that he had a cyclonic temper. When soon afterwards Ford suggested that O'Malley put in a good word for his cousin Martin Feeney to enable him to be awarded an IRA pension, O'Malley did not let sentiment or friendship cloud his vision. He told Ford that he had not seen active service with Feeney and therefore would have to leave the task of recommendation to those who had.

Later in 1956 when Ford returned to Ireland to film *The Rising of the Moon* he again engaged the services of Ernie O'Malley, this time as "technical adviser". On this occasion there was probably more substance to his role because one of the three segments of the film based on Lady Gregory's play *The Rising of the Moon*, and called simply *1921* in Ford's production, concerned the escape of a Republican prisoner sentenced to death during the final stages of British rule in Ireland. This of course closely mirrored events in O'Malley's own life. Ford still valued his friendship immensely and was comforted by his presence on the set.

Fittingly, and in contrast to *The Quiet Man*, O'Malley's name appears prominently on the screen credits as

Technical adviser: Earnán O'Malley

using the Gaelic form of his christian name.

Sadly, at this stage O'Malley was quite ill and died the next year, 1957. He had endured jail, torture, a hunger strike, and still carried in his body fragments of the bullets that had caused his severe wounds dozens of years previously. In later years he was often in Ford's thoughts. When Ford, now very ill himself, returned to Ireland in 1964 to direct part of *Young Cassidy*, he asked as if in a time-warp – "Who was at Ernie O'Malley's funeral? Did they do the right thing by him? Did he get military honours?" By this time, O'Malley had been dead for over seven years.

It is both surprising and regrettable that Ernie O'Malley's exciting and adventurous life has not been the subject of a feature film. An excellent drama-documentary shown on Irish television (RTÉ ONE) on 25th November 2003 about his daring escape from a secret room in a suburban Dublin house gives just a taste of how exciting a film about his life could be. As Richard English has pointed out, O'Malley was a great admirer of the Scottish novelist John Buchan and his hero Richard Hannay, whose adventures he read while in prison. Though O'Malley was Irish, Catholic and a Republican anti-Imperialist, and Buchan a Scottish, Presbyterian and Tory Imperialist, the two shared a love of adventure, the thrill of being chased, and the desperate resourcefulness of a man on the run from the forces of law and order. Like Richard Hannay, O'Malley was buzzed by an airplane on the wilderness of a Celtic hillside. John Buchan's classic *Thirty Nine Steps* has been filmed in four different versions (with a fifth promised recently) – O'Malley's real-life adventures were just as exciting as the fictional Hannay's.

The McLaglen Family

Sean Thornton (John Wayne) lands a punch on Red Will Danaher (Victor McLaglen) during the big fight while local extras look on.

Top: Red Will Danaher (Victor McLaglen) tells his sister Mary Kate (Maureen O'Hara) to leave the room while Sean Thornton (John Wayne) and Michaeleen Óg Flynn wait hopefully for good news about their marriage proposal.
Bottom: Red Will (Victor McLaglen) gives Sean Thornton (John Wayne) a free drink while barman Pat Cohan (Harry Tyler) looks on alarmedly.

Top: Peace and quiet at last come to Inisfree. The brother-in-law (Victor McLaglen) joins Mary Kate and Sean for supper.
Bottom: Michaeleen Óg Flynn (Barry Fitzgerald) and Sean Thornton (John Wayne) bid against Red Will Danaher (Victor McLaglen) to buy White O'Morn from the Widow Tillane (Mildred Natwick).

Top: Victor McLaglen obliges with an autograph at Ashford Castle for Aidan O'Carroll.

Middle: Andrew McLaglen, paymaster, hands out the daily wages to Quiet Man extras near Ryan's Hotel in Cong.

Bottom: Andrew McLaglen, son of Victor, and Assistant Director of The Quiet Man chats with a member of the wardrobe department beside the Playfair house.

Bottom left: Arthur Shields, Andy McLaglen and Tom Carman (sound man) with hat.

Chapter Six

O'Máille's and The Quiet Man Costumes

Costumes are yet another virtually unnoticed aspect of a film – in *The Quiet Man* they blend in so well with the background and locations that we have to consciously look for them before we see them. John Ford's ancestors came from Galway and Mayo – Spiddal, Connemara, Dunfeeney and the Aran Islands, so the costumes used in *The Quiet Man* were strongly influenced by the traditional style of clothes worn in the West of Ireland. These included Aran sweaters, bobailín caps, crioses (traditional Irish woollen belts), black and coloured Galway shawls, Irish tweed suits, coats and waistcoats.

Striving for authenticity, Lord Killanin advised Ford to engage the services of a family firm that was then and still is, Ireland's premier designer and maker of traditional Irish costumes – O'Máille's of Dominick Street, Galway (now located in 16 High Street, Galway). This family retail business was founded by Pádraig O'Máille (O'Malley in Anglicised form) as far back as 1938. He was joined by his brothers and sisters in building a strong trade in hand-tailored coats, jackets and suits for both men and women – these were worn by everyday people and were quality garments at affordable prices. Pádraig assembled a talented group of tailors and seamstresses who plied their trade in separate parts of the Dominick Street premises – seamstresses on the ground floor, tailors upstairs, all under the watchful eye of Mary (Ciss O'Máille).

Stiofáin O'Máille wearing a traditional Irish costume provided by O'Máille's of Galway.

The Killanin family had enjoyed the O'Máille's hand-tailored suits and jackets and respected the family's expertise in handling Donegal tweeds. Many yards of hand woven tweed were required for the splendid suit worn by Squire Danaher. Dan Tobin was resplendent in his cape of wool/frieze and trousers tailored in Kelsey (boiled natural wool). Mary O'Máille took responsibility for Maureen O'Hara's wardrobe, travelling to Ashford Castle to carry out the fittings for her outfits, conveyed in style in a Rolls Royce. The simple sewing machine, a Singer Hand-

Duke Wayne and Andy McLaglen, son of Victor, model some beautiful O'Máille costumes.

Machine, on which she worked is still displayed with pride at the family store at 16 High Street, Galway.

Bríd O'Máille, the wife of Sean O'Máille, was chosen to tailor the children's clothes for the Race Day at Lettergesh. Those scenes were of course filmed in Hollywood, so the costumes travelled across the Atlantic.

The cast of *The Quiet Man* built up quite a rapport with the O'Máille family and Maureen O'Hara in particular enjoyed the friendship of Pádraig and Stiofáin O'Máille. In June 1988, when Maureen was conferred with an honorary doctorate by the National University of Ireland at University College Galway, Mary and Bridie O'Máille were invited guests and enjoyed a reunion with Maureen and her family, who were regular visitors at O'Máille's store.

Duke Wayne caused a sensation when he arrived at O'Máille's in Dominick Street shopping for bolts of tweed in 1951. It was lunchtime and word quickly spread among local schoolboys that the world's greatest cowboy had arrived in the City of the Tribes and the West of Ireland. Duke was mobbed, but with great presence of mind, he put his hand in his pocket, extracted a generous handful of coins and scattered them in all directions. This action distracted his urchin fans and he made good his escape. Incidentally, it is said that the hard hats worn by Wayne and Barry Fitzgerald in *The Quiet Man* were supplied by a firm owned by Maureen O'Hara's father Charles Fitzsimons.

Pádraig O'Máille was the first retailer in Ireland to sell the now world famous Aran Sweaters and sixty-five years on the business thrives under the ownership of Seán O'Máille's son Gerard and his wife Anne (to whom I am indebted for information and photographs). The O'Máille shop in Galway is an essential stopping place for all visitors to Ireland. Recently O'Máille's featured on the Oprah Winfrey TV channel Oxygen, aimed at women viewers, and so achieved worldwide fame. The O'Máille website at www.omaille.com/ is well worth a visit.

The Quiet Man cast model the wide range of traditional Irish costumes designed and made by O'Máille's of Galway. Left to right at back are Francis Ford, John Wayne, Victor McLaglen and John Ford. In front sits Barry Fitzgerald. The picture was taken in Ashford Farm in front of the Farragher house, which was the Danaher house in The Quiet Man.

Locations - Past and Present

Left and bottom: Some scenes from the races on Lettergesh Beach. Is Wayne directing?
Below: Thoor Ballylee north of Gort, Co. Galway, where Mary Kate and Sean ran across the river. It was previously the home of Irish poet W.B. Yeats.

Above: A splendid view of the Widow Tillane's house (now demolished) in the grounds of Ashford Castle.

Left and right: The sheep stars of The Quiet Man, filmed on the Ashford Deerpark.

Above: *Dan Tobin's house in 'Blazes Lane' Cong, from which the old man miraculously emerged to watch the fight.*
Below: *The legendary Caisléan Circe (Hen Castle) which appears in The Quiet Man.*

The courting scene on the jaunting car Sean Thornton (John Wayne), Michaeleen Óg Flynn (Barry Fitzgerald) and Mary Kate Danaher (Maureen O'Hara) at Ashford Farm.

Filming Sean Thornton's arrival at Inisfree in front of Pat Cohan's Bar.

Right: Barry Fitzgerald rests and Wayne waits opposite Pat Cohan's Bar.
Top left: The footbridge in front of White O'Morn where Michaeleen and Sean first viewed his old home.
Below left: Father Paul (James Lilburn), Mary Kate Danaher (Maureen O'Hara) and Father Lonergan (Ward Bond) film on the streets of Cong.

The main street in Cong (Inisfree) opposite Cohan's Bar today. The dog is the direct descendant of a dog appearing in The Quiet Man!

Left: Left to right, in front of the replica Quiet Man Cottage in Cong, Margaret Collins, Bill Maguire (double for John Wayne) and Gerry Collins.
Middle: The bedroom in Collins' Quiet Man Cottage in Cong.
Right: Robert Foy, extra in The Quiet Man who drove the cart across the river, pictured with author Des MacHale at the launch of The Complete Guide to The Quiet Man at the Collins' Quiet Man Cottage in Cong.
Bottom: The delegates at the second Quiet Man fan club meeting at Ashford Castle, September 2003.

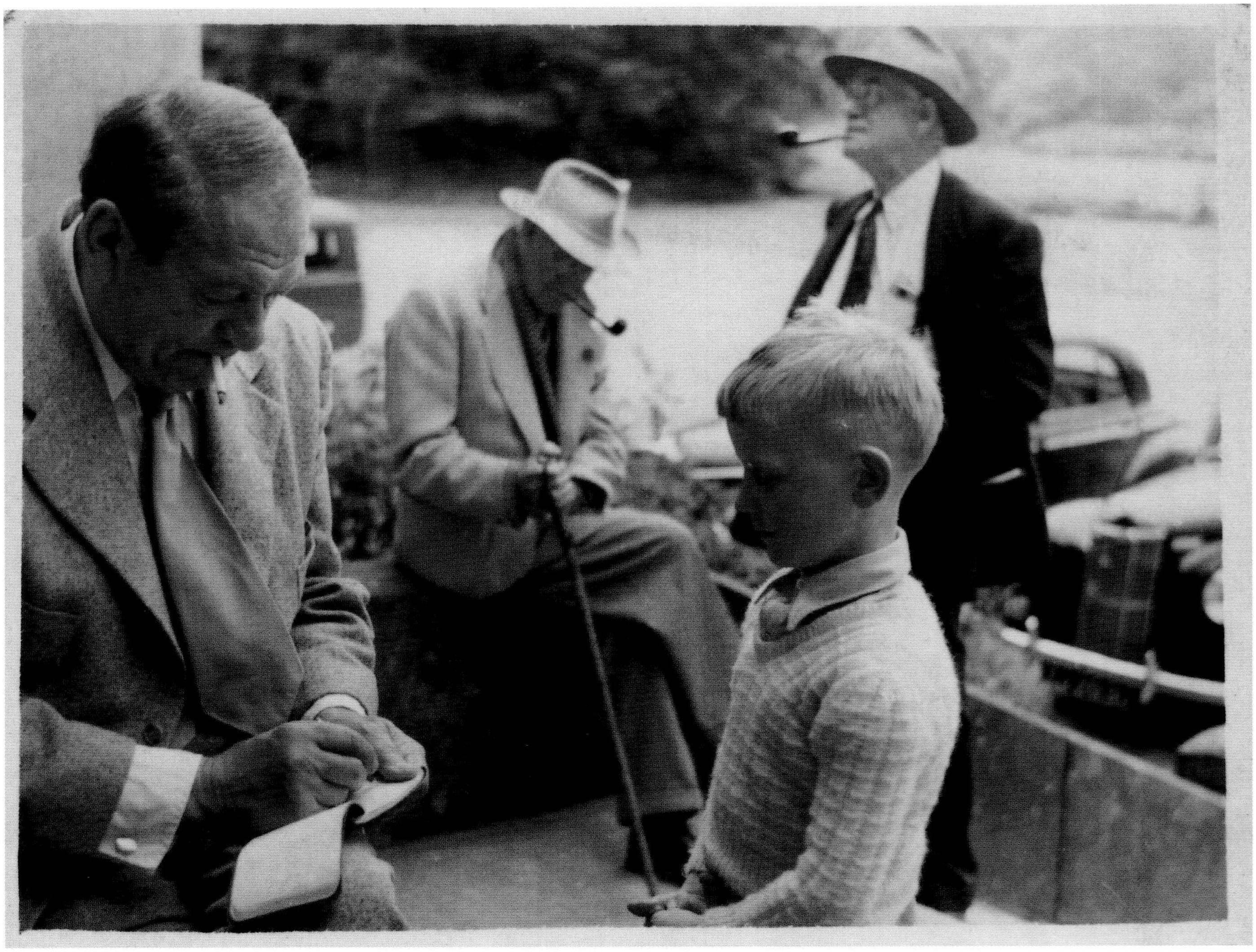

Victor McLaglen signs an autograph at Ashford Castle for an admiring young fan. In the background are, left, John Ford and right, his brother Eddie O'Fearna, both keen pipe-smokers.

Chapter Seven

Trouble in the Glen (1954)

As any author or film-maker will tell you, if you write a successful book or make a successful film, the publisher or producer will immediately look for a follow-on, a sequel or just more of the same money-making formula. In CGQM we have already discussed several *Quiet Man* clones including *Happy Ever After* (1954), *The Rising of the Moon* (1957) and even *The Field* (1990), but there was another very blatant attempt to ride on the back of the success of *The Quiet Man*, produced by Herbert J. Yates whose financial backing had made the original possible in the first place. It was called *Trouble in the Glen* (1954), which the author has seen only just recently for the first time and which is well worthy of examination, if only as a terrible warning.

Trouble in the Glen (1954) was, like *The Quiet Man*, produced by Herb Yates' Republic Pictures Corporation and one can almost imagine the board of directors asking "How can we have another hit movie and keep the money rolling in?" First, they must have asked if this guy Maurice Walsh had written any other stuff – what, nearly two dozen best-selling novels? Surely there must be the basis of a hit movie among them, but which one to choose? Walsh had for many years lived in Scotland and several of his novels were based there; why not choose one of them with lots of heather, drams of whisky, lochs, kilts, highland scenery and all the rest of it and do for Scotland and people of Scottish descent worldwide what *The Quiet Man* had done for Ireland? Eventually Walsh's novel *Trouble in the Glen*, written as late as 1950, was chosen; the important fact that *The Quiet Man* was based essentially on a short story of Walsh's rather than a full-length novel was disregarded.

Herb Yates, Boss of Republic Pictures Corporation, whose money eventually made The Quiet Man possible.

Next, how many of the *Quiet Man* team could be persuaded to take part in the new project? John Ford, after his very unhappy financial experiences with Yates had vowed never to work with him again and never did. But Frank Nugent, whose sparkling screenplay had contributed so much to *The Quiet Man*, was willing to adapt Walsh's novel for the screen and that was a huge start. Vic Young, whose musical arrangements did so much for the overall *Quiet Man* atmosphere also came on board, another huge acquisition. Of the acting stars only Victor McLaglen, visibly older and looking rather unwell, took up the offer. There was no question of Duke Wayne or Maureen O'Hara offering their services for the deliberately small fees they had agreed for *The Quiet Man* out of friendship for Ford, so substitutes had to be found. So why not dress Forrest Tucker up in a check cap? He looked a bit like Wayne and perhaps the gullible moviegoers would not be able to tell the difference. For the female lead, the well-known actress Margaret Lockwood was chosen, frosty and distant and with an undisguised English accent to boot.

But the biggest casting stroke of all was the signing of the great Orson Welles as the Laird of the Glen, newly arrived in Scotland from South America to claim his heritage with a dusky complexion that owed more to boot polish than the sun. As one critic has remarked, the sight of the huge Welles in a tartan kilt in the final scene was on its own worth the admission charged to see the film. Actually, though *Trouble in the Glen* was shot in Perthshire in Scotland, all of the scenes involving both Welles and McLaglen were shot in Hollywood studios, with very obvious backdrops and back projection. Welles freely admitted that he took the part just for the money and McLaglen at times looks as if he did too. Finally, the fact that TRUCOLOR was used rather than Technicolor certainly did very little to bring out the beauty of the Scottish scenery which of course in reality matches that of the West of Ireland.

Trouble in the Glen was co-produced and directed by the Englishman Herbert Wilcox of Wilcox-Neagle Productions. Wilcox was married to the famous English actress Anna Neagle, but he resisted the temptation to cast her in the leading female role. From start to finish the film is a blatant *Quiet Man* imitation, incorporating as many incidents and aspects of its predecessor as the wafer-thin plot would allow. The credits first feature a bank of heather to set the tone but soon dissolve to a scenic lake. An American in a check cap arrives in a little Scottish village which he left many years ago and stands drinks in a Cohan-like pub on the corner, where the barman, played by Eddie Byrne, wears a bowler hat. A lovely lady herds cattle on horseback, while the American, smoking a cigarette, falls in love with her. There is a bishop visiting the big house for reasons that are totally irrelevant to the plot. Margaret Lockwood wears a bobailín hat very like that worn by Maureen O'Hara and Forrest Tucker utters a half sentence that nearly gives the game away before he bites his tongue. There is a token bit of Scots' Gaelic on a notice – Thá an rathad so duinte le ordugh uachdaráin – which poor old Forrest Tucker has a half-hearted attempt at pronouncing, and of course there is a big punch-up at the climax. There are several open cars and fights with the biggest fish ever taken from the loch. Naturally there are snatches of *Quiet Man* dialogue peppered throughout the hour and a half of screen time.

Yes, there is actually a plot of sorts revolving around the fact that the road through the Glen is closed by the laird after he has been insulted by a gillie and the tinkers (led by McLaglen) rise up against this. A subplot concerns a little girl Alguin (played rather convincingly by Margaret McCourt) fighting against polio. However, the overall impression is almost farcical and one can imagine the entire cast just waiting to collect their cheques and run. But the single most astonishing aspect of *Trouble in the Glen* is the appalling monologue delivered by the scenery-chewing Welles (who actually began his acting career in Dublin) at the beginning of the movie, in which he insults Scotland and the Scottish people in a most unsubtle way. One feels that the very first rule of movie-making is not to insult your target audience and if the intention was to be funny, it fails miserably. One shudders to think that the great Frank Nugent wrote this kind of stuff – let us hope that he did not and that this speech came from some other source, perhaps Welles himself. A sample of the monologue should illustrate the point:

> This is Glen Echan – we are high in the Highlands (or Heelands) in an area infested with tribes of hostile savages known as Scotsmen and situated a good many degrees north of civilisation...That awful old man you can see coming over the hill is a member of my clan... When this uncle of mine nine times removed or indeed any of his fellow barbarians break into the local version of human speech, what you hear is a wild series of grunts and snorts known as a "burr"...A man could get more peace among the headhunters of the Amazon. You know it's a matter of historical fact that the bagpipes were actually invented by the Moors and brought back to Europe after the Crusades. The rest of the world very soon got fed up with this frightful caterwauling but here we are ten centuries later in Scotland and they're just getting started. The Roman Empire, which of course brought civilisation to the rest of Europe never even managed to get into this country. Caesar took one look and gave up...

When one considers how much of a fuss Herb Yates made about the one word "national" in *The Quiet Man*, it seems little short of amazing that he allowed the insulting drivel just quoted to be used in *Trouble in the Glen*.

What then was lacking in *Trouble in the Glen*, which went nowhere at the box office and has since vanished almost without trace? The principal missing ingredient was of course the direction of John Ford, although it is doubtful if even he could have done much with it. But he would certainly have spiced up Nugent's screenplay a bit with cuts and additions and perhaps curbed Welles' excesses. Sadly, Vic Young's music was in this instance flat, dull and unmemorable – surely Ford would have included some of the hundreds of beautiful Scottish melodies to give character and depth to the action. But at very least *Trouble in the Glen* can serve as an awful warning about happens when the opportunity of making a motion picture falls into the wrong hands and is made purely for profit rather than for artistic reasons.

As for Maurice Walsh himself, it was yet another unhappy experience with movie-making. Immediately after the success of *The Quiet Man* in 1952, he had authorised his publishers Chambers to negotiate with Republic Pictures for the sale of the film rights of *Trouble in the Glen*, suggesting a fee of £5000 (sterling), soon reduced to £3000. Walsh, quite justifiably, argued that he had been misled over the fees for the highly successful *Quiet Man* and that he should be adequately paid for this next film. After a long series of suspicions and misunderstandings, Walsh settled for a sum of just under £4000, but the process left a bad taste in his mouth and this was his last involvement with movie-making. This was a pity, because he had several later offers from more amenable sources. He refused to act as assistant in the Scottish locations of *Trouble in the Glen*, being far too sick and tired of the whole business to take any further part in it. For the record, when the movie of *Trouble in the Glen* appeared, he disliked it heartily. In contrast, Maurice Walsh was on the set of *The Quiet Man* in Cong several times and very much approved of the film.

Victor McLaglen indulges in a cigarette during time out at Ashford Castle. He was the only actor from The Quiet Man *who took part in* Trouble in the Glen.

The Action Begins…

Feeney (Jack MacGowran) looks on while Red Will Danaher (Victor McLaglen) enjoys a celebratory drink after selling the crossbreds in Inisfree, helped by local extras.

Sean Thornton (John Wayne) lands a punch on Red Will Danaher (probably double Martin Thornton) in the big fight at the hay field on Ashford Farm.

"Well give a man a hand then". Sean Thornton (John Wayne) graciously helps Red Will Danaher from the water while a host of bit players and extras look on. Fourth from the left is the famous Irish boxer Martin Thornton.

"Here's a fine stick to beat the lovely lady." The Fishwoman (May Craig) hands Sean Thornton (John Wayne) a weapon with which to chastise his wife Mary Kate (Maureen O'Hara).

A break in the big fight outside Cohan's Bar. Michaeleen Flynn (Barry Fitzgerald) tells Sean Thornton (John Wayne) that the betting is even money. Behind from left are May Craig, Paddy O'Donnell and Joseph O'Dea. In front, left to right are Joe Mellotte, Bill Maguire (stand-in and double for John Wayne respectively), Paddy Hopkins and Robert Foy.

Above: The drag begins at Castletown Station. Extra John Horan is on the left.
Below: Burning Passion

Chapter Eight

A Quiet Man Miscellany

Fans of *The Quiet Man* are insatiable in their demand for bits and pieces of interesting information about their favourite movie and its stars. In this chapter I have gathered together such a pot-pourri, a miscellany, a collection of trivia, call it what you will. If you wish to add to it, I would be delighted to hear from you.

★

Philip Stainton, who played the part of the Bishop, was known for many years afterwards as "the Bish". It is said that he emerged from the *Quiet Man* set dressed in his Episcopal regalia and was met by two nuns who immediately knelt down and kissed his ring, mistakenly believing him to be a real bishop. After his triumphant procession through the cheering crowd towards the end of *The Quiet Man*, Stainton remarked, "I was probably the first Englishman to be cheered by Irishmen in Ireland. To show there were no hard feelings I shouted "Up the Republic". Incidentally, a local newspaper in July 1951 asked pointedly why Lord Killanin had not been cast in the role of the Bishop. He certainly looked the part!

Father Peter Lonergan (Ward Bond) with electrical engineer Paddy Lydon in Cong.

Later Stainton went on to star in Ford's *Mogambo* (1954) and who can forget him as the kindly policeman in *The Ladykillers* (1955).

★

At least one member of the cast of *The Quiet Man* appeared in *Gone With the Wind* (1939). It was Ward Bond. Now have another look at that classic movie and see if you can spot Father Lonergan in there doing his stuff!

★

Among those originally suggested for the part of Sean Thornton in *The Quiet Man* was Hollywood actor Robert Ryan. Ryan had some boxing experience and, as his surname indicates, he was of Irish extraction. I don't think he would have had the same impact as Duke Wayne in the part.

★

Sean Dunphy, one of Ireland's most popular singers, who represented his country in the Eurovision Song Contest so successfully (remember *If I Could Choose*?), is a really big *Quiet Man* fan. He collects *Quiet Man* photographs and memorabilia and has even built a little White O'Morn replica in his back garden. When he tours the United States, *The Isle of Innisfree* is requested so often that it has become a permanent number in his repertoire.

★

Duke Wayne wore a hairpiece throughout *The Quiet Man* except at the beginning of the fight scene when his cap fell off. His hair started to fall out after he contracted a virus in Korea.

★

Vic Young, who arranged the music for *The Quiet Man* so beautifully, was nominated for an Oscar or Academy Award no less than eighteen times but never won this top prize during his lifetime. Then in 1956 he was nominated for the nineteenth time for the Oscar for Best Scoring of a Dramatic or Comedy Picture for his contribution to *Around the World in 80 Days*. Sadly, Vic died four months before the ceremony but won the Oscar posthumously. He wrote the scores for over three hundred movies, among which were *For Whom the Bell Tolls* (1943), *Frenchman's Creek* (1944), *The Paleface* (1948), *Shane* (1952), *The Country Girl* (1954) and of course *The Quiet Man* (1952).

★

Duke Wayne's epitaph is written in Spanish. Translated, it reads:

He was ugly, he was strong, and he had dignity.

★

Andrew V. McLaglen, son of Victor, was an uncredited Assistant Director on *The Quiet Man*. He went on to become a full director of big scale westerns in later life. Among his credits are *McLintock!* (1963), with Wayne and O'Hara; *The Rare Breed* (1966); *The Undefeated* (1969) and *The Train Robbers* (1973).

Victor Young who arranged the music for The Quiet Man. *After many nominations he was eventually awarded the Oscar he so richly deserved.*

★

Gabriel Byrne, Ireland's current movie superstar, is also a big *Quiet Man* fan. He devotes a chapter to the movie in his autobiography *Pictures in My Head*.

★

Would you believe that a Sesame Street character was inspired by a *Quiet Man* actor? It was the puppet Bert based on Ward Bond's character in the TV series *Wagon Train*. Now look closely; surely you can see the resemblance? Incidently, in another twist, Ward Bond appeared as Police Officer 'Bert' in *It's a Wonderful Life*, playing opposite a taxi-driver character called 'Ernie'!

★

James Lilburn, who played the part of the curate Father Paul, was of course Maureen O'Hara's brother, James Fitzsimons. He took his screen name from his mother's maiden name, Lilburn. There was another contender, however, for his part as the curate in *The Quiet Man* – Harry Carey Jr. (Dobe), but perhaps an American parish priest and an American curate would have been too much for the fans to swallow.

James Lilburn afterwards appeared in *Suddenly* (1954) with Frank Sinatra, about an assassination attempt on the President of the United States. This is the movie that Lee Harvey Oswald is reputed to have watched before he shot President John F. Kennedy.

James Lilburn appeared as a costermonger in *My Fair Lady* (1964) and appeared with his sister again in *The Rare Breed*. In later years he changed his name to James O'Hara and worked with Joel McCrea, the well-known director of many Westerns.

★

The churches at Cong were not the only ones filmed for *The Quiet Man* – two scenes were shot at other churches but they fell victim to cutting room economies. John Daly, of equestrian fame, relates that the original "patty-fingers in the holy water" scene was shot at Clonbur Church just a few miles away from Cong. He was there, in charge of Barry Fitzgerald's horse. However, at a crucial stage, a donkey "misbehaved" and it was too late to reshoot the scene because of failing light. So the Clonbur location never made it to the final cut.

Left: The beautiful "Harry Clark" stained glass window in the Catholic Church in Cong which appeared in The Quiet Man. Right: The Church of Ireland in the grounds of Ashford Castle where the "patty-fingers" scene was shot.

★

While he was in Cong, John Ford told the story of how the family name changed from Feeney to Ford. His brother Francis had run away from home to join the film business at a time when it was not as respectable as it is today. Fearing his parents would trace him, and perhaps also to spare their blushes, Frank decided to change his surname but couldn't think of a suitable choice. He happened to look out a window and saw two cars – a Ford and a Cadillac. Quipped John, Frank chose Ford because he couldn't spell Cadillac!

★

Nothing was left to chance during the filming of *The Quiet Man* in Cong. The set had to be as quiet as Duke Wayne himself. On one occasion the big cameras were in action when the sensitive sound equipment picked up the vibration of a heavy motor in the distance. It transpired that some tractors were operating about two miles away. The owner of the vehicles was given £2 for each of them to stop the noise for an hour. (Tractors sound like actors!)

Early in the morning on another occasion everything was in readiness for shooting a street scene when the ever-vigilant Andy McLaglen noticed that no smoke was coming from a certain chimney. The owner of the house was awoken and asked if he would light a fire. Straw and jute bags were ignited and a realistic effect achieved. The house owner received £1 for his trouble.

⋆

Ward Bond, dressed in the clerical garb of Father Lonergan, was strolling in the grounds of Ashford Castle when he met a visiting priest. The real priest asked what parish and dioceses "Father" Bond was from and wondered if they had any mutual friends, as he knew many American priests. Bond replied that he was stationed in the Dioceses of Hollywood and knew Father Bing Crosby and Father Spencer Tracy very well. However, the priest was not a movie-goer and the names meant little to him. Bond finally revealed the deception.

⋆

Local newspaper reports of 1951 indicate that many women and children from the village of Cong were hired to make crowd scenes for the wedding of Sean and Mary Kate which was staged in a disused Protestant church. This scene, which apparently was shot, did not make it to the final cut.

⋆

A reporter and photographer from the *Connacht Tribune* newspaper in Galway were dispatched to Cong to interview and photograph the stars. Naturally they took the scenic route and arrived rather late in the evening. Ford was in a large tent on the lawn at Ashford and sent Duke Wayne to see who the arrivals were. Wayne returned and told him "They say they're from the Chronic Turbine".

⋆

A few *Quiet Man* bloopers or "oops" moments recently spotted by the author:

(i) Sean Thornton and Michaeleen Óg Flynn meet Father Lonergan on their way to Inisfree and engage in conversation with him. They then proceed at full pace to Inisfree, the sidecar being drawn by Napoleon. And who is there chatting on the street when they arrive? None other than Father Lonergan, who does not seem to have a car or any other means of conveyance. Now how did he manage that?

(ii) When Dermot Fahy begins to play the *Wild Colonial Boy* on the melodeon he is not wearing any headgear but when the camera cuts to him a little later, without any break in the music, he is suddenly wearing a bobailín cap of the type popular in Connemara. If he didn't take his hands off his instrument, who put the cap on his head?

(iii) When Sean and Mary Kate wish to escape from the attention of Michaeleen as a prelude to their romp through the countryside in the courtship scene, he asks her "Can you ride a bike?" Can't he remember that he met her riding a bike just a few scenes earlier when he addressed her, "Hello, Mary Kate Danaher".

⋆

In the year 2002, the leader of the Conservative opposition party in Great Britain, Ian Duncan-Smith, fighting for political survival, described himself as a "quiet man". For weeks afterwards, almost every British newspaper carried pictures of Wayne and O'Hara and the movie *The Quiet Man* enjoyed a huge revival. (Actually, *The Quiet Man* has always been a favourite on BBC television, endlessly repeated, especially on Saint Patrick's Day). Sadly, Ian Duncan-Smith lost his battle to remain leader of the opposition and was replaced by the less quiet Michael Howard.

⋆

One of the most remarkable feats of athleticism in *The Quiet Man* is Father Lonergan's vaulting of the gate in order to get to the fight more quickly. However, it appears that Ward Bond was given a little help to overcome gravity. A frame by frame examination of the scene will reveal that he leaps from a carefully constructed little platform inside!

⋆

We have already recounted in CGQM several jokes which Ford implanted in *The Quiet Man*, little realising that video and DVD technology would catch up with him. Here is another: before the race scene, Mary Kate and Wayne's children sit on a cart which of course is a studio scene. Some writing is visible on the cart and with very great difficulty it has been deciphered by zooming in on the DVD version. It reads:

A.J. HOLMES, DUBLIN,

a joke on the custom of Irish farmers putting their names on the shafts of their donkey carts. Ace Holmes (no relation of

Sherlock's) was of course the propman who acquired this and many other artefacts for the movie.

★

One of the greatest scandals of the movie business is that the lovely Maureen O'Hara was never awarded the Oscar which her many great performances so richly deserved. Even more incredibly, she was never even nominated for an Academy Award, despite winning dozens of other awards. In 2004, the author, on behalf of *The Quiet Man* Movie Club, wrote to the Academy of Motion Pictures earnestly requesting that a Lifelong Achievement Oscar be awarded to Maureen O'Hara, a beautiful and dignified lady who has brought credit to her profession. He cited her performances in *The Quiet Man* (1952), *How Green Was My Valley* (1941), *Miracle on 34th Street* (1947), *Spencer's Mountain* (1963), *The Parent Trap* (1961), and *Jamaica Inn* (1939).

★

There were many people involved as scriptwriters before the final version of *The Quiet Man* emerged. The original short story was of course written by Maurice Walsh in three versions – one for the *Saturday Evening Post*, another for *Chambers' Magazine* and a third as a chapter in his novel *Green Rushes*. There is an unconfirmed story that Liam O'Flaherty, author of *The Informer* on which another Ford Oscar winner was based, was also involved at some stage, but this seems unlikely. Then Richard Llewellyn turned the story into a novella which was rejected on the grounds that it was too political – this was not Llewellyn's fault, because that was the brief he was given. Finally Frank Stanley Nugent stepped in and, with a few nudges from Ford, wrote the screenplay of the final version. Recently, however, another person has been mentioned by Joe McBride as having done some work on the screenplay of *The Quiet Man* before Nugent. He was American scriptwriter Laurence Stallings (1894-1968). Having co-written *She Wore a Yellow Ribbon* (1949) and *The Sun Shines Bright* (1952) for Ford around this time, it is certainly quite possible that he was called in to assist on *The Quiet Man*.

The pillars outside the Ashford Church that have recently been stolen. We want them back at once!

★

In 2003, in an act of unprecedented sacrilege, blasphemy and vandalism, a highly organised gang removed, under the cover of darkness, the tops of the stone pillars at the gateway of the little Church of Ireland in the grounds of Ashford Castle. These pillars of course were the very ones that appeared in *The Quiet Man* as Mary Kate listened to the two men discussing her lack of a fortune, so the motive for the theft could have been only cinematic. Stonecutting equipment was used and no trace of the perpetrators was ever found by the police. If you were involved in this theft and are reading this, please ensure that this part of Ireland's movie history is returned to its rightful place immediately!

★

In Autumn 2003, the author, in a vain attempt to escape from *The Quiet Man* for a short period, decided to take an adult education course in Astronomy at University College, Cork. An excellent course it was too, conducted by Galwayman Dr. Paul Callinan. One of the many topics I became interested in was comets, those beautiful icy objects that orbit the solar system, so I consulted a book containing the details of all known comets. Guess what? There is a comet called Inisfree! I wonder if ET has ever landed on it? It seems you just cannot get away from this movie - even in space!

★

Patty Joubert e-mails me from the USA to inquire if Fitchburg, Massachusetts is the home town of Sean Thornton in *The Quiet Man*. Sorry, Patty, great try, but the original screenplay has Pittsburg, Massachusetts, USA, a splendid joke about Michaeleen's sketchy geography, and designed no doubt by John Ford to make US audiences feel superior. But doesn't it show the lengths to which people will go to see if their home town Fitchburg can grab a mention in the world's greatest movie!

★

The start of the big race. From left, Hatswell, Quinn, Pat Ford, Lilburn, McLaglen and Wayne.

I received another delightful e-mail from Kathy and Randy Vernam of Oregon USA, full of interesting snippets of *Quiet Man* information. In particular they tell me:

> The saddle used by John Wayne in *The Quiet Man* is actually a McClellan saddle, not a cowboy saddle. It is an American cavalry saddle used in the army in the 1800's. No cowboy would use such a saddle because it has no horn! A western stock saddle, or cowboy saddle, requires a saddle horn to dally to. It would be very dangerous for a cowboy to use a saddle with no horn.

★

Finally, an e-mail from another *Quiet Man* fan Roy Pitkin, in which he puts me right on a couple of statements I made in CGQM. Although John Wayne suffered initially from lung cancer, Roy tells me that the cause of death was actually stomach cancer. Also, I stated that John Ford was given the "Congressional Medal of Honor" by Richard Nixon. Roy states that this should have been the Medal of Freedom, recognition for a variety of accomplishments but sometimes with political implications, given by the President.

Glad to set the record straight and thank you Roy!

★

That great film director Jim Sheridan, who directed *The Field* (1990), is a big *Quiet Man* fan. On December 2003, according to newspaper reports, he revealed that he wants to make an all-black version of *The Quiet Man* with African actors. He claims that Djimon Hounsou, who plays a tortured African artist dying of AIDS in his latest movie, *In America* would be perfect for the John Wayne role.

I can't see it happening myself, Jim. And anyway, why tamper with perfection?

★

All over the world, there are currently nearly a hundred cinema museums devoted to various aspects of cinema history, from the Laurel and Hardy Museum in Ulverston, Cumbria (birthplace of Stan Laurel) to the Gene Autry Museum of Western Heritage, Los Angeles. *The Quiet Man*, however, appear to be the only individual movie that has a museum all to itself. This is of course the *Quiet Man* Heritage Centre, Cong, Co. Mayo, the site of which actually appears in the film as the Bishop's car comes round the corner to be greeted by hundreds of Catholics "cheering like Protestants" in the closing scenes.

The *Quiet Man* Heritage Centre, which is run by Margaret and Gerry Collins and their family, is a perfect replica of White O'Morning and a visit there is a must for any *Quiet Man* fan visiting Ireland.

★

In 1957, the English dramatic critic, Kenneth Tynan, who had Irish blood in his veins, wrote to J.P. Donleavy, the American author residing in Ireland, concerning a story and film script entitled *The Rich Goat* which Donleavy had submitted to Ealing Films Limited, in outline form. Tynan wrote:

Dear Mike (Donleavy's nickname),

Before you embark on your story for us, I thought I ought to pass on to you a very minor qualm that someone here has raised. Did you ever see a film called *The Quiet Man*, directed by John Ford? It is a story about a rich American who goes to an Irish village to live in the cottage where his mother was born. She has just died and he has inherited it. He falls in love with an Irish girl and has a tremendous fight with her brother, a village bully. I think it would be as well if your story avoided any obvious parallels with Ford's.

Otherwise, go ahead and *ad lib*. I'm looking forward to the result with enormous gusto.

Love,
Kenneth Tynan.

Two days later, Donleavy replied that he was "delighted with qualm". He did remember vague roses, sunny curtains and shouts round a cottage in emerald fields. He gave his assurance that there would be no parallels, not even in the colour of the grass. In the event *The Rich Goat* never made it to the screen and perhaps the story was never written. It seems what happened to Donleavy is commonplace among authors – they read a book or see a movie and later rewrite what they saw, sincerely believing it to have come from their own imagination.

★

When Brendan Met Trudy (2000) is a quirky film starring Peter McDonald and Flora Montgomery, set in Dublin, with screenplay by Roddy Doyle. Brendan is a wimpish schoolteacher obsessed with old movies, in particular those directed by John Ford. Early on in the film, it shows him in a modern Dublin cinema and guess what is showing? You guessed it – it's *The Quiet Man* – the scene where Mary Kate screams when she sees her reflection in the mirror and Sean kisses her as she attempts to run out of the cottage. As he watches, Brendan mumbles to himself – "How does he do it?" – but it is not clear if he is referring to Ford or Duke Wayne. Other clips from Wayne and Ford include *The Searchers* (1956) and *The Man Who Shot Liberty Valance* (1962), and there is also a clip from William Dieterle's *Hunchback of Notre Dame* (1939) which starred Maureen O'Hara.

When Brendan Met Trudy is an inoffensive and undemanding film not without moments of pleasant comedy, but it leaves one question unanswered – why is a mainstream Dublin cinema showing *The Quiet Man* in 2000?

★

Part of the fun of watching *The Quiet Man* again and again is the discovery of "oops" moments, bloopers, breaks in continuity, or just downright mistakes, call them what you will. We have already mentioned three of these but here are a couple more.

(iv) When Red Will Danaher enters the bar to take Sean to task for buying "his" land and for the attention Sean is paying to Mary Kate, observe Will's tie closely. The pattern changes several times during the scene, indicating that it was taken off and put back on again several times, but in a slightly different position each time.

(v) When Michaeleen is delivering Sean's proposal of marriage to Mary Kate they go inside because the sun is too warm – it is completely dry outside. Once they go inside, however, large raindrops are clearly visible on the window behind them.

★

In CGQM we pointed out that there were many "echoes" i.e. incidents that happen earlier in the movie that are mirrored by incidents that happen later. Here are a few more of those echoes.

1. Before the race, Fr. Paul's mother kisses her son on the forehead as she blesses him and warns him to ride safely. Later, as Elizabeth Playfair says goodnight to her husband Cyril, she too kisses him on the forehead.

2. Mary Kate is so excited by the arrival of her furniture at the cottage that she jumps over the crib without waiting to remove it. Later when she is being dragged from the station, she jumps over several trunks and boxes.

3. Early on in the movie, Mary Kate angrily questions Sean, "And who gave you the right to be kissing me?" Later on, the enraged Sarah Tillane puts the hapless Will Danaher in his place with, "And who gave you the right to make such an announcement?"

★

In the original Maurice Walsh story, the character played by Francis Ford is called Matt Tobin; in the movie he becomes Dan Tobin. One wonders if the reason for this is that in *Woman of the Year* (1942), Spencer Tracy informs Katherine Hepburn that he has given a character called Dan Tobin a champagne-bottle "christening". Or maybe it's just another Fordean coincidence.

★

One of the more intriguing theories about *The Quiet Man* is that the whole movie is, like 'Alice in Wonderland', merely a dream in the mind of Sean Thornton, perhaps when he lay flat on his back in the boxing ring after being floored by an opponent. The movie certainly has a dreamlike quality and many of the characters that appear are just the sort of people one would encounter in a dream. Sean's arrival at Castletown Station and his first encounter with the locals has all the hallmarks of a nightmare where he cannot make himself clear or find the way to Inisfree. His first sight of Mary Kate is a dream of a much more pleasant sort and he even questions her reality by saying, "Is that real? She couldn't be".

I look forward to some devoted *Quiet Man* fan writing an extended essay or maybe a thesis on this interesting question!

★

Here is an additional line of dialogue that occurs in *The Quiet Man* but was not recorded in CGQM. It is: "And that's a fact".

Who says it? In what part of the movie? Quiet Maniacs, get to your VCR and DVD machines at once and find out for yourselves!

★

When Michaeleen says to Mary Kate, "You've got a tongue like an adder", perhaps he forgot that there are no snakes in Ireland (except in Dublin Zoo!). Saint Patrick drove them all out over fifteen hundred years ago.

★

Sean Thornton is wearing a wedding ring when he arrives in Castletown, but does Mary Kate wear a wedding ring at any stage after marriage? Just another question to be investigated. And can you spot her wearing a real-life wedding ring before her marriage in the movie?

★

Just a few years ago the DVD version of *The Quiet Man* was released. Initially, there were some complaints about the trueness of the colours, but the clarity of the picture is spectacular and for that alone it is worth buying. There are several worthwhile extra features, but be careful about one of them – the English subtitles. These approximate only very roughly to the actual dialogue and there are many blunders and phonetic renderings and downright hilarious guesses.

Initially I had intended listing them all in this book but considerations of space prevented this; but if you want a good laugh and you know the dialogue well, have a look for yourself.

★

There are versions of *The Quiet Man* in French, German, Spanish, Italian and several other languages worldwide. Some years ago the author suggested that there should be a version in the Irish language Gaelic, not least because the movie already contains several sentences in Irish as well as being shot very close to the Connemara Irish speaking area, an Ghaeltacht. In 2004 as a result of consultations with Udarás na Gaeltachta, TG4, the Irish language television station, aided and abetted by Mr. Paddy Rock, this project has got off the ground and we hope to have an Irish language version of *An Fear Ciúin* in the near future.

★

Here are some additional names to add to the list of *Quiet Man* extras in CGQM:
Maureen O'Flaherty and Bríd O'Flaherty (Cousins of John Ford's from Spiddal); Kay Naughton and her father.

★

When Red Will Danaher throws Mary Kate's fortune in gold coins on to the table he calls out proudly, "Three hundred and fifty pounds gold", but if you take the trouble to count the coins, as I have done, you will see there is no way that they could have made up that amount. Each coin would have been a gold sovereign, worth one pound and there certainly were not 350 of them. Is this another case of the bully Red Will attempting to short change his sister?

★

This is getting a bit ridiculous – the latest film to jump on the *Quiet Man* bandwagon is *Kill Bill: Vol. 2* (2004) which I have just learned from the wonderfully useful Internet Movie Data Base contains a scenario from *The Quiet Man*. At this rate, *The Quiet Man* will go on to establish a new record – the movie from which a scene is shown in the most other movies.

★

Further media reports indicated that James Bond star Pierce Brosnan was to marry in the "*Quiet Man* Church" in Cong. Not quite true – Widower Brosnan was married in Ballintubber Abbey, Ireland's oldest church in continuous use since the thirteenth century, about twenty miles away from Cong. However, the reception was held at Ashford Castle, the luxurious hotel where so many *Quiet Man* scenes were shot.

★

Richard Llewellyn, one of the early scriptwriters on *The Quiet Man*, pulled quite a fast one on the literary world in general and John Ford in particular. According to newspaper reports in 1999, Llewellyn (real name Richard Lloyd), author of *How Green Was My Valley*, was born in London, not in Wales and never worked as a miner. He was not raised in the mining community of Gilfach Goch, but in Hendon, North London, the son of a Welsh-born hotelier. His first job was as a hotel dishwasher and it is doubtful if he was ever down a mine in his life. What he knew about mining he learned from his relatives and his only real connection with Wales was when he bought a farm in Pembrokeshire. Sadly, he was declared bankrupt in 1947 and spent the rest of his life abroad, before dying in 1983. But his book and the film based on it were masterpieces and persuaded Ford to let him have a go on *The Quiet Man*. Maybe he knew about the deception – isn't that what movies and literature are after all?

A celebratory dinner for the cast and crew of The Quiet Man *in Ashford Castle at the end of the filming.*

Barry Fitzgerald and Arthur Shields - Quiet Brothers

Michaeleen Óg Flynn (Barry Fitzgerald) tells Mary Kate Danaher (Maureen O'Hara) that she has a tongue like an adder as he prepares to deliver Sean Thornton's proposal of marriage.

Above: Michaeleen Óg Flynn (Barry Fitzgerald) warns Sean Thornton (John Wayne) to keep his mouth shut during the matchmaking negotiations with Red Will Danaher.
Below: Michaeleen Óg Flynn (Barry Fitzgerald) asks Mary Kate Danaher (Maureen O'Hara) if she goes for it.

Two Oscar-winners sit side-by-side on set in Cong - Archie Stout and Barry Fitzgerald.

Barry Fitzgerald - the loveliest and kindest of men takes a rest between takes.

Above: Stand-ins Joe Mellotte (for John Wayne), Jim Morrin (for Barry Fitzgerald) and Etta Vaughan (for Maureen O'Hara) prepare for the courtship scene.
Right: Barry Fitzgerald learns his lines in the Deerpark at Ashford on the set of The Quiet Man.

Left: Arthur Shields at Ashford Castle – well prepared for a shower. Below: Barry Fitzgerald lies on the grass in Cong next to Lord Killanin while Chata Wayne indulges in a quick cigarette.

Above: Quiet Man stars wait for a bouquet from John Ford riding in the Bishop's car. Included are Wayne J., O'Hara, Wayne M., May Craig, O'Dea, O'Donnell, Overlander and assorted extras.

Left: Giving or taking – The Reverend Mr. Playfair (Arthur Shields) and the Bishop (Philip Stainton) betting on the big fight.

Right: Barry Fitzgerald and his brother Arthur Shields take time out for a smoke with the local policeman in Cong.

Brotherly love - Barry Fitzgerald and Arthur Shields waiting for the cameras to roll.

Barry Fitzgerald clowns about dressed as a railwayman. The others are, from left Joseph O'Dea, Eileen Crowe, Eric Gorman and May Craig.

Barry Fitzgerald's double drives the jaunting car through Cong – Etta Vaughan and Maureen O'Hara are on the right.

Chapter Nine

Quiet Man Bit Player Identification

The stars of any motion picture are nowadays always credited at the beginning of the movie and, in the old black and white films one thankfully sees so often on the television, they are credited at the end as well. In more recent times, the main players and the director are credited with the opening titles, and a very extensive list of all the technical crew and support is given at the very end, this list often lasting for five minutes of screen time. These lists of credits are now almost ludicrously detailed and if *The Quiet Man* were to be remade today (God forbid!) one could expect a credit reading

Miss O'Hara's tea stirred by...

or maybe even worse.

Cliff Lyons, who played the second Judge at the races; he was a regular Ford bit-player.

Nevertheless, there still remains a good deal of work to be done with regard to the identification of bit players in *The Quiet Man*, and this is where you, the reader, can make a genuine contribution to research on the greatest movie of all time. But first, the good news – since the publication of CGQM, two important bit players have been conclusively identified, although they have not been included in any published or unpublished cast list that I have seen.

1. The first of these identifications is the second judge at the horse race for the Inisfree Cup, shot on Lettergesh Beach. The first judge is played by veteran Ford bit player, Major Sam Harris (the General!) but now we can reveal that the second judge is played by another old Ford favourite, CLIFF LYONS. All of the scenes in which Cliff Lyons appeared were of course Hollywood studio shots and he did not travel to Ireland for any of the location scenes.

Cliff Lyons appears in several *Quiet Man* scenes and is given quite a few lines to speak. We first see him before the race with his binocular case strapped over his shoulder, pinning Sean's colours on while saying "Your colours, Thornton". Next, wearing his distinctive hat, he wishes Sean "Good luck", before escorting the Widow Tillane to the finishing line. It seems that Cliff Lyons' job is to record in his copybook the names of the ladies who

Left: Ward Bond poses in clerical garb in Cong.
Middle: Feeney (Jack MacGowran) in thoughtful mood.
Right: Quiet Man Assistant Director Albert Podlansky poses with Ward Bond in Ashford.

Part of the race course at Lettergesh Beach which featured in The Quiet Man

are putting up their bonnets for the Inisfree Cup, so as the Widow Tillane puts her bonnet in position on the stake, he courteously bows in her direction. Next, he nods to Dan Tobin's daughter and swaps some doubtlessly witty banter with Dan himself, before finally graciously exchanging bows with Mary Kate, who has finally been goaded into putting up her bonnet.

During the race, which the two judges follow throughout with their binoculars, Sam Harris shouts "Foul, Guppy", to which Lyons does not respond. Later, Harris shouts "Foul, Father Paul" (what a suggestion – that a Catholic curate would cheat in a race even if it meant boosting parish funds; why, it's almost on a par with suggesting that a Playfair would cheat at tiddlywinks!) but Lyons turns on him rather sharply and says "I didn't see it!". Presumably if the alleged infringement was not seen by both judges then no further action can be taken. A reader has e-mailed me (and I really love *Quiet Man* related e-mails – keep them coming to d.machale@ucc.ie) with the ingenious suggestion that Cliff Lyons is meant to be Father Paul's father and this is why he is reluctant to penalise him. Well, why not? Father Paul's mother, Mae Marsh, is prominent in the movie, and wouldn't these two old Ford stock players make a lovely couple? Unfortunately, there is no evidence in the script one way or the other, and in fact the judges were a late studio addition to the screenplay; so there the speculation will have to remain. Finally, Cliff Lyons is prominent among those celebrating Sean's victory in the horse race.

Cliff Lyons was born Clifford William Lyons in South Dakota in 1901 and died in Los Angeles in 1974. Sometimes credited as Cliff "Tex" Lyons, he appeared in nearly a hundred movies often directed by Ford or starring Wayne and almost always as a bit player. Starting as a sherriff in *West of the Law* (1926) he appeared in, for example, *Three Godfathers* (1948) (Guard at Mojave Tanks); *She Wore a Yellow Ribbon* (1949) (Trooper Cliff); *Wagonmaster* (1950) (Sheriff); *Rio Grande* (1950) (Soldier), *The Searchers* (1956) (Colonel Greenhill); *Two Rode Together* (1961) (William McCandless) and *O'Donovan's Reef* (1963) (Australian Naval Officer).

But Cliff Lyons was to play a more important part in movie history. He was an expert stuntman and stunt double for such stars as Anthony Quinn, Tyrone Power and Henry Fonda, and in his later years a stunt consultant and stunt co-ordinator in such films as *How the West Was Won* (1962), *McLintock!* (1963) and *The Train Robbers* (1973). Around 1947, when Ford was making *Fort Apache* (1948), the Society for the Prevention of Cruelty to Animals succeeded in banning the tripping of horses in movies using hidden wires. Lyons developed a safer, more humane method of staging horse falls by training them to fall on cue from the rider. This technique became standard practice and must have saved the lives of hundreds of animals that would otherwise have to be put down even if they had been only injured.

Elizabeth Playfair (Abbey actress Eileen Crowe)

Lyons also played a part in what has almost become part of movie folklore. When Harry Carey, whom Ford made a star but who also helped to make Ford a great director, died in 1947, Ford felt he should pay him a lasting tribute. Carey's son, Harry Carey Jr. (Dobe) was starring in *Three Godfathers* (1948) and before the final scene was shot, Ford mysteriously sent him home. Then Cliff Lyons, dressed up like Harry Carey, rode Carey's horse up the crest of a hill, stopped there and looked into the sunset. The opening credits of *Three Godfathers* featured that scene and the dedication:

TO THE MEMORY OF HARRY CAREY
BRIGHT STAR OF THE EARLY WESTERN SKY

Finally, Lyons displayed yet another talent as Second Unit Director or Assistant Director on such movies as *She Wore a Yellow Ribbon* (1949), *Rio Grande* (1950), *The Alamo* (1960), *The Green Berets* (1968) and *Big Jake* (1971). He was truly a remarkable man of many parts and a worthy cast member of *The Quiet Man*.

2. When Sean Thornton enters the bar of Pat Cohan's public house to introduce himself to the common people of Inisfree, there are several other men drinking in the bar already. Among them are Pat Cohan himself (Harry Tyler), Dan Tobin (Francis Ford), Dermot Fahy (Ken Curtis) and bit players Frank Baker (with cap and pipe) and Pat O'Malley (grey-haired man with pipe). There is another man there with a black moustache and

Sean Thornton (John Wayne) buys drinks for the locals in Inisfree. On the left is Dan Tobin (Francis Ford, brother of John Ford) and in the centre is Pat Cohan, barman (Harry Tyler).

wearing a hat and trenchcoat. He advances towards the bar and sings the *Wild Colonial Boy* lustily with the others. When Red Will Danaher enters and begins to criticise Sean for buying the land he himself longs to own, our friend in the hat and trench coat suddenly berates him:

"And if you were half the man you think you are, you wouldn't begrudge a Thornton the right to his own birthplace".

The man in question has been conclusively identified as COLIN KENNY. His real name was Oswald Joseph Collins and he was born in Dublin in 1888. He died in Los Angeles in 1968 just a couple of days short of his 80th birthday. During a long and varied career he appeared in nearly a hundred movies, almost always as a bit player and more often than not as a policeman, a detective or just a man

Pat Cohan's Bar today. The grocery store will soon be converted to a real bar.

Dubliner Colin Kenny, a man in the pub, sandwiched between John Wayne and Ward Bond.

in the background. He appeared in two Tarzan films (1918), *Little Lord Fauntleroy* (1921), *Bonnie Scotland* (1935) with Laurel and Hardy and *Dr. Jekyll and Mr. Hyde* (1941). In 1942 he was a policeman in the Oscar-winning *Mrs. Miniver* – Maureen O'Hara of course was to star as Mrs. Miniver in one of her greatest television roles. Sadly, Colin Kenny's many parts were almost always uncredited and his name appears on the screen only a handful of times. But he was a very solid and reliable bit player and now is famous forever because he has been identified as having a speaking part in *The Quiet Man*.

Well, so much for the successful identifications, but how about those who remain? Who for example are Danaher's three workmen who sit at dinner table with their backs to the corner? Who is the little man with the cap holding one of the horses before the race? Who are

Packy is served dinner by Maureen O'Hara while Feeney (Jack MacGowran) looks on.

the other customers in the bar? What actors play the parts of the wedding guests and the drinks waitresses? Who are the pipers at the race and the policemen in the boxing ring? And who on earth is the man in the closing scenes pretending to be Guppy? It would be satisfying, if not vital, to identify all of these people and doubtless in years to come names will be put to some of them.

However, there is one other unidentified bit player who has caused the author many sleepless nights over the last fifteen years. All efforts to identify him, both amateur and professional have so far failed, so we collect here all the known information about him in the hope that some reader may be able to break the deadlock – autographed copies of the author's books on *The Quiet Man* will gratefully be sent to anybody who makes an authentic identification.

The actor in question plays the character of Packy MacFarlane, one of Danaher's workmen. He sits at the dinner table facing the camera and he has a speaking part. "My dad remembers his dad well, Mike Thornton, he had shoulders on him like an ox", he says, spreading his arms. From his accent, the actor is very probably American and he appears in Ford's *The Long Gray Line* (1955) where he plays a bit part of a West Point soldier who sits on a bench during the football match. When Donald Crisp sits on the other end of the bench, the soldier is forced off and has to sit on the ground looking annoyed.

Red Will Danaher mentions him by name when trying to buy the Widow Tillane's field:

'Shure,' I said to him, 'Packy MacFarlane, you'll never make me believe that Sarah Tillane would be selling White O'Morn.'

That kindly man Harry Carey Jr. (whose book on Ford, *Company of Heroes* is strongly recommended) when contacted wrote me a lovely letter apologising for the fact that he could not identify the actor though he too appeared in *The Long Gray Line*. Maureen O'Hara, who appeared with him in both *The Quiet Man* and *The Long Gray Line*, could not remember who he was either. Those excellent professional bit part identifiers John Cocchi, Ken Jones, David Quinlan, Simon Rose, Jack Dewesberry and Brian Downes who have been so helpful to me in so many other cases also drew a blank in this case. So, reader, please identify this actor and grab a piece of fame for yourself!

Incidentally, Packy MacFarlane was the name of a well-known boxer in the US in the twenties and thirties; clearly this is another in-joke.

Do you know this man?

Making The Quiet Man

Ford in the thick of the action at Ashford Farm

The scene at Ashford Farm as the cast prepare for the courting scene.

Above left: This backs up the claim that Duke Wayne did a little of the directing of the race at Lettergesh Beach while Ford was ill.
Above right: Local political celebrities visit the shooting of The Quiet Man in Cong. Left to right, we have Ward Bond, Canon Carney, three unnamed politician, Barry Fitzgerald, Victor McLaglen and James Lilburn.
Below left: John Wayne with Mrs Ivan Howe centre and Lady Killanin outside the Playfair House in Cong.
Below right: Duke Wayne with fan Patricia Mooney.

Maureen O'Hara has her make-up applied by her make-up man Jimmy Barker at Ashford Farm during the making of The Quiet Man.

A view of the courting scene at Ashford Bridge.

Left: The lighting crew in action.
Above and below: The elevated camera crew on Lettergesh Beach wait for the race horses to arrive.

Right: An unidentified wardrobe man on The Quiet Man team carries out his duties. Below: Lighting, cameramen, film crew and production assistants wait at Lettergesh and Teernakill.

The courtship scene near the Playfair house.

How the Playfair greeting scene would have looked on screen without the cameras and lights.

Right: Barry Fitzgerald takes a rest from the film action in the hayfield at Ashford. On the left is Ashford Manager Noel Huggard with his hands behind his back; on the right are Paddy O'Donnell and Charles Fitzsimons.

Above centre: The mechanics of filming on the bridge near the Playfair house. Note the camouflage on the camera on the left.

Below centre: Unidentified Stand-in is ready to pounce as the Playfairs wait for the action.

Left: Ford's Girl Friday, Meta Sterne, keeps an eye on the script and production at Ashford.

Chapter Ten

Eye-Witness Accounts

Over the years many myths and legends have grown up around *The Quiet Man* and its shooting so that at times it is hard to distinguish fact from fiction and truth from fantasy. One way of getting round this difficulty is to talk to people who were there and in whom one has absolute trust that their accounts are authentic. So in this chapter I have gathered together a number of eye-witness accounts based on interviews or letters requested by me. I am very confident that all of these accounts are genuine descriptions of what happened way back in 1951.

Charles J. Harold

Charlie Harold, geologist, archaeologist, opera lover, Christian gentleman and dear friend, was one of my indispensable researchers when writing CGQM. He was Assistant Manager to Noel Huggard at Ashford Castle during the filming of *The Quiet Man* in 1951 and was there for the duration of the shooting. Indeed he inadvertently appeared as an extra in the movie – during his lunch break one afternoon he wandered down to Ashford Farm where the "Let the courting commence" scene was being filmed. As he sat on the wall watching the scene being rehearsed, Ford shouted "Don't nobody move – roll the cameras" and Charlie Harold is to be seen in the final cut sitting on the wall in one of the most beautiful scenes in *The Quiet Man*. Charlie Harold took a great number of photographs of the action, some of the very few in colour, and several of these appear in both CGQM and *Picture The Quiet Man*. Here are some of his recollections about the great events in Ashford Castle in 1951:

The stars of The Quiet Man stop for a chat in the grounds of Ashford Castle during shooting.

It was in Autumn 1950 that we first heard at Ashford that the cast and crew of *The Quiet Man* were coming to stay with us. Around that time John Ford, Lord Killanin and Ward Bond visited Ashford Castle, but to the best of my memory, did not stay. Charles Fitzsimons stayed at Ashford during the filming, but not beforehand as far as I know.

In those days, Ashford was very popular with anglers and although the film people took over our entire premises, they did not discommode our "Mayfly Regulars" who had just finished their sport and departed.

The provision of food for the movie stars and crew was one of our most important functions; they seemed very happy with the cuisine we provided except for the fact that they liked to make their own salad dressing rather than use our mayonnaise. They ate lamb, home-grown on Ashford Farm, and beef from our butcher Mr. Divilly which came from the Aran Islands and was marbled with fat. To sustain them for the hard work of location filming they had a full Irish breakfast consisting of sausage and bacon (from Castlebar), egg, boiled and scrambled, with coffee and marmalade. On workdays there was no breakfast in bed – they were up at 7.30 am and on the road at 8:30. With them they took packed lunches – cold meat, salad, cheese, biscuits and several kinds of fruit - apples, oranges, pears and bananas. When they returned in the evening they had dinner between 6 and 8 and the choice of main courses included beef, lamb, chicken, (Castlemahon) salmon and trout from nearby Lough Corrib and from Mr. Barber of the Galway Weir. Angela Huggard and Mary Brown baked homemade Irish Bread to die for, and Ward Bond was once allowed to bring a lobster he had acquired to the kitchen to be cooked to his specification. John Joe Mullins was on breakfast duty and

The beautiful grounds of Ashford Castle in 1951. Much of The Quiet Man was shot there but the castle itself appears only in the opening credits as Ford thought it was a bit "grand"

delivered early morning tea at 6am to those who wished to rise early (too early perhaps). The story that Victor McLaglen was driven regularly to Tuam because it was the only place he could get a decent steak is a very dubious one, because Ashford had a reputation for the excellent quality of their steaks. Meat was properly hung at Ashford and there was a good selection of sea fish available also including turbot and cod. But no chips or French fries were provided.

Etta Vaughan, stand-in and double for Maureen O'Hara, with the sisters Neva Bourne (Wardrobe) and Fay Smith (Hairdressing).

The manager Noel Huggard took personal responsibility for the choice of menus and took a particular interest in soups, fresh Irish vegetables grown on Ashford Farm, and desserts. Homemade consommé and traditional chicken soup using stock were his speciality. Vegetables were simple but delicious – carrots, lettuce, potatoes, spring onions and cabbage were supplied in abundance but there were no exotic vegetables in evidence. Desserts were nearly all homemade by cook Mary Brown (there was no chef) and included trifles, apple tart, blackberry tart, crepe suzette, chocolate mousse, queen of puddings, with cheese to follow. No attempt was made to serve traditional Irish dishes such as boxty, potato cakes or colcannon. Post-war food rationing was not a problem.

Ashford Castle in 1951 had twenty-two double

The Wayne family arrive in Ireland. Chata and Duke are at the back; in front are (l to r) Michael, Melinda, Patrick and Toni.

Time out on the lawns at Ashford during the shooting of The Quiet Man. Wayne, O'Hara and the Bishop (Philip Stainton) are clearly visible.

rooms and three singles and these were all occupied, some by the camera technical crew. John Ford was polite and friendly and there were no outbursts of temper from him. He wore a cap and a patch over one eye; he smoked a pipe throughout his stay and his favourite snack was Mrs. Mullin's toasted wholemeal bread. Ford could be a bit irritable but he was always pleasant and during the six-week period of the filming he was sober at all times. There was no filming on Sundays, their day of rest, and Ford and many others went to Mass each Sunday. There was little time for entertainment or singing – after dinner most

people just went to bed around nine o'clock to prepare for the next day's filming.

There was some evidence of a little coolness between John Ford and his brother Frank – they were rarely seen talking together while at Ashford. And relations between John Ford and the manager Noel Huggard definitely did deteriorate as time passed. Huggard felt that the American film people were too demanding and were taking over his hotel. At the end of their stay, it does appear as if Ford and Huggard were not on speaking terms. And finally, Ford was not laid up for four days with illness, allowing Duke Wayne to direct the race scenes – Ford missed only half a day through illness.

John Wayne, his wife Chata and Wayne's four chil-

Above: Ford relaxes in Connemara with Maureen O'Hara and his Girl Friday Meta Sterne.
Below: A meeting of the members of the "Young Men's Purity, Total Abstinence and Yachting Association" held near Spiddal Pier in County Galway. Delegates are, from left to right, Ward Bond, John Ford, Pat Ford (John Ford's son), John Wayne and Eddie O'Fearna (John Ford's brother).

dren stayed at Ashford Castle – he was friendly and undemanding and everybody called him "Duke". There were not as many bathrooms as he and his family would have liked and there was always a huge rush for the showers in the morning; the water was heated by a hopper feeding sawdust by the lorry load from the local sawmills into a burner operated by local man Mick Varley. The Wayne children ran around the Castle as children do, but they were well-mannered and polite. Duke Wayne smoked regularly – indeed his stand-in, local man Joe Mellotte was deputed to have his favourite brand of cigarettes on hand at all times. Drinks available in the Pigeon Hole bar at the hotel included Irish whiskey, gin, port and bottled Guinness. Wayne did drink a little but rarely to excess. On one occasion he was forced to drink some of the lethal local brew poitín by Martin Thornton and as a result had to be carried upstairs to bed.

Maureen O'Hara was very pleasant and easygoing and had no special needs. She had a special nurse to look after the needs of her daughter Bronwyn Bridgid who had recently made her first Holy Communion just before her seventh birthday. Sometimes Maureen's singing teacher from Galway would arrive and Maureen would sing at the piano. She and Ford attended Mass together on Sundays in the local church in Cong but nobody can recall them ever speaking Irish together. Maureen O'Hara's personal driver was local man Tom Ryan.

The overall impression at Ashford was that the cast and crew of *The Quiet Man* were very pleasant people who worked extremely hard at their demanding jobs. Victor McLaglen was good-humoured, but "rough and ready" and was kept strictly in tow by his son Andy. Ward Bond was friendly at all times but Barry Fitzgerald could be a bit cantankerous at times especially when deprived of his pipe. Although generally a very lovable character, Barry suffered from ill-health while at Ashford and this fact may have accounted for his moodiness. Arthur Shields, Eileen Crowe and May Craig all stayed at Ashford and were exceptionally nice people as were Archie Stout, Winton Hoch, Tom Carman, Lee Lukather and Albert Podlansky. Meta Sterne, Ford's Girl Friday, was an extremely strong-willed character who protected Ford from all potential problems and abuse. She was "the boss", the woman in charge and she knew just what she wanted at all times.

The beautiful Ashford Castle from the air in whose grounds much of The Quiet Man was shot.

Finally, there were many other staff at Ashford (about thirty local people were employed there) and in Cong who played their part in the background for the successful making of *The Quiet Man*. There was Jack Murphy who drove the second unit to Clifden and elsewhere; Paddy O'Donnell who ferried the completed film to Shannon Airport; Peggy Clark who served in the bar; head gillie Jim Costello and gillies Jim Morrin and Stephen Lydon, who also acted as doubles and stand-ins.

The weather at Ashford was good for the filming period with only just a little rain. On Sunday, their day of rest, the cast and crew often enjoyed touring and exploring the local area; the now extensive mail for Ashford was collected in a sealed bag by the porters each weekday morning from Mary Diskin and Mrs. Gibbons at the post office; the single telephone line from Claremorris was

The tower at Ashford Castle where many of the stars' bedrooms were situated.

expanded to many just for the film people; and of course *The Quiet Man* caused electricity to be brought to Cong for the first time.

ADDENDUM

In a short interview, Jack Murphy owner of Pat Cohan's Bar, in April 2004, strongly asserted that he drove Victor McLaglen several times to the Imperial Hotel in Tuam so that he could enjoy a decent steak. "And", added Jack, "He never left me outside!" Jack also confirmed that he drove doubles Bill Maguire and Etta Vaughan to Clifden and Kylemore and that it was they, rather than Wayne and O'Hara who featured in those long shots.

Monsignor Joseph Maguire

A VISIT TO THE SET OF *THE QUIET MAN* IN HOLLYWOOD, L.A., IN AUGUST 1951

In August 1951, during a trip to the USA, I visited Los Angeles. I stayed for a few days in a Parish House with a priest friend who had been my class fellow in Maynooth (1943-47).

In response to my wish to see a film being made, he brought me on one of those days out to the Republic Studios in San Fernando Valley. He had made arrangements with John Ford, with whom he was friendly, for us to visit the set of a film on which the famous director was working. I had no idea what I was going to see nor whom I was going to meet.

We arrived in mid-morning and were passed through the security. Eventually we were brought to meet the great man. He received us most graciously. On recognising the *fáinne* I was wearing, he conversed very fluently in Irish for some time and then in English. He told me that he and his colleagues had been in Ireland recently and that they had had a marvellous time. They had been filming outdoor scenes of a film in the West of Ireland and were presently shooting the indoor scenes. I had not heard of *The Quiet Man* until then.

The film set was located in a huge open hangar-style building. The first item that caught my eye was a prominently-placed "Irish cottage" with whitewashed walls and freshly thatched roof. Behind it covering the whole of the very expansive wall was a painting of an Irish countryside. The landscape was of fields of green with winding roads and limestone walls throughout them.

The work in progress when we arrived was of the reception for the wedding of Sean Thornton and Mary Kate Danaher.

Over to the side of the hangar the party was assembled for the wedding photograph. My recollection is of the two or perhaps three rows of guests with the bridal couple sitting together in the middle of the front row.

It was then that I met John Wayne. His double was standing in for him. He and I walked up and down in the vast arena for about an hour. Occasionally he was called back to be filmed. We chatted about Ireland and he was most enthusiastic about the great time he had had there. He was extraordinarily friendly, a charming person you would think you had known all your life. He was a large man, dressed for the wedding like the countrymen I knew in Ireland at Mass on Sundays, in a double-breasted suit of navy blue. My clearest memory of our conversation was when he caught me by the lapel of my jacket and said, "I know what that is", referring to my Pioneer pin, "I have a score of friends here who could be doing with one".

The next person I met was Maureen O'Hara. Somehow I was speaking again to John Ford and he said to me, "Have you met O'Hara yet?" He called her over from among the wedding-photo party. She came towards me, a tall lovely smiling young woman arrayed as a bride. Her most striking feature was the sheen of her dazzlingly-bright red hair. Her demeanour was friendly and modest.

At this stage too I met Ward Bond, who, if I am not mistaken, was the Parish Priest in the film. He impressed upon me his admiration for the Sisters who had nursed him in a recent bout of illness in their hospital.

My next memory is of joining the company for lunch. We sat at a wide table outside the "Irish" cottage. I have no recollection whatsoever of what was on the menu. I was so enthralled sitting next to Barry Fitzgerald. My impression of him was that he was a weary, tired little man. He told me he longed for the peace and quiet of home. He said, "You might think that this country has everything, but I wish I was back in Ireland". I also met his brother Arthur Shields. He was very much the gentleman I admired as the Reverend Mr. Playfair. Eileen Crowe was there too, a gentle, friendly lady who poured the coffee.

As far as I can remember, it was after lunch that they shot the scene of the maid bringing in the tray. This took a lot of time. Ford asked the girl to walk across the room about half a dozen times. During this scene he called for silence several times. Someone said to me, "You're seeing the tough side of the director now, God help anyone who moves or speaks when he calls for quiet".

My next recollection was the singing of *The Humour Is On Me Now* to the accompaniment of the piano or harmonium played by one of the two Fitzsimons (Maureen O'Hara's brothers). The device they used was of him (dressed, I think, as a young priest, with Roman collar) playing the instrument. In reality the music was being played by someone in a corner off camera.

My final recollection was of walking with my friend, who had come back to collect me, into the brilliant Californian sunshine with the sound echoing throughout the courtyard of *I will and I won't get married, for the humour is off me now*. It was an unforgettable experience.

I have seen the film more than a dozen times since then. The most memorable occasion was on the Isle of Barra in the summer of 1958. It was a ramshackle parochial hall in Castlebay where they had just one projector and the packed audience stamped the floor in rhythm to the céilí music that was played during the intervals.

I often marvel at the industry that is involved in film-making. I had been there for about six hours and the scenes I saw went by almost in the twinkling of an eye in the completed picture.

Philomena (Lorigan) O'Hara

Below is my recollection of visiting Ashford Castle during the filming of *The Quiet Man* in July 1951.

A classmate friend, long dead, and myself, visited a relative of hers in Dublin, after the graduation ceremony at UCC. A family member there, a priest, was going to Clifden, for a family christening. We were invited to go along and we were delighted. Before taking the boat!

The weather happened to be fine and the sun was shining. On the way, our driver asked if we would like to stop for tea and needless to say, we said yes! We did – at Ashford Castle. My recollection is of a large foyer, full of people – we were in blissful ignorance of what was happening and no-one bothered us; nowadays we would probably be asked to leave.

My next recollection is of being in a large dining room – we were the only occupants – the tables covered with white cloths. We were served by a tall, gaunt, elderly silent man, wearing a white apron. Elderly, that time was estimated against my own age. Afterwards, my friend and self went to the ladies' powder room – I recollect going upstairs – we were engaged in animated euphoric type conversation – so our glance towards the tall man coming down was casual and brief. He looked, curiously, at us and that was it. I vaguely, fleetingly, recognised him – probably because I was City and would possibly have seen a film of his – my friend was from the Country and perhaps wouldn't. We continued with our conversation, uninterrupted by any reference to this man – the *Quiet Man* – John Wayne.

The Ladies' Room was very interesting – in fact, I think it may have been communal (both sexes!) and very much what one would associate with a castle.

We left the Castle – again the weather was still pleasant and sunny. In retrospect, I would say the road surface was a "dirt type" road like a refined type of bohareen. So dust was in plentiful supply!

I recollect coming towards us a stretch limo/large car. I recollect seeing Maureen O'Hara, who looked beautiful and was smiling. Because of the road surface – each car tended to sway, but we did not impact. Ballinrobe Races were on that day, so the occupants of the other car were possibly there, as they looked very happy – probably had backed the right horses.

We then travelled on to Clifden.

Philomena (Lorigan) O'Hara

It is remarkable that, after 52 years, I can recount that visit to Ashford Castle – July 1951. Like a black and white photo of all above – then put aside lying dormant all those years – then suddenly recollected – when *The Quiet Man* continues to generate interest, curiosity and nostalgia, plus all the visitors coming to the area, especially Americans. Plus, again, all that went on in my own life, when the world was my oyster. And the relatively early death of this friend who was - to me - from that lyrical place, Knockeenacutting Macroom.

An *Quiet Man*
Le Mike P. Ó Conaola

Ba i Samhradh na bliana 1951 a rinneadh an scannán *The Quiet Man* in iarthar na hÉireann and cé gur iomaí scannán a rinneadh in Éirinn ó shin níor sháraigh aon cheann acu an stádas atá bainte amach ag an scannán seo a bhfuil a cháil ag dul i mead ar fud an domhain ó bhliain go bliain. Tagann na mílte turasóirí go Conamara agus go Maigh Eo gach Samhradh d'aon turas leis na háiteanna ina ndearnadh an scannán a fheiceáil – Caisleán Ashford ar theorainn na Gaillimhe agus Mhaigh Eo, an stáisiún traenach "Castletown" i mBéal Átha Glúinín, suíomh an tí ceann tuí "White O'Mornin" ar an Mám, droichead na Léime taobh thiar de Uachtar Ard, Baile Chonga áit a raibh "Pat Cohan's Bar" agus áiteanna go leor eile atá le feiceáil fós morán mar a bhí siad gan athrú ón Samhradh álainn grianmhar sin 1951.

Bhí áiteanna eile ar nós An Spidéil a raibh baint mhór acu leis an *Quiet Man*. Sa Tuar Beag taobh thiar den Spidéal a saolaíodh Athair John Ford. Sé John Ford an stiúrthóir cáiliúil as Hollywood a rinne an scannán. Ba as an mbaile fearainn sin a d'fhág Seán Ó Feinneadha nó Seán Mháire le dul go Meiriceá i 1872 in aois a shé bliana déag gur lonnaigh i mBoston i dtosach agus ansin Portland, Maine. Is ansin a casadh a bheanchéile, Bairbre Ní Churraoin air. Tháining Bairbre as an gCoill Rua. Níl idir an Tuar Beag and An Choill Rua ach cúpla mile bealaigh ach ní feasach dom go raibh aithne acu ar a chéile sa mbaile. Phós said thall agus thóg siad aon duine dhéag clainne. Ba é John an té ab óige – John Aloysius Feeney a d'athruigh a ainm go dtí Ford nuair a thosaigh sé ag plé leis na scannáin. Rinne a dheartháir Francis an rud céanna blianta roimhe sin. Tá ballaí an tí inar rugadh athair John Ford ina seasamh i gcónaí sa Tuar Beag.

Tá gaolta go leor le John Ford i gceantar an Spidéil. Col cúigireacha le Ford iad muintir Fheinneadha as an Tuar Beag – Beartla, Pádraic agus Ned Ó Feinneadha atá i gcónaí taobh thiar den Spidéal ar an gCnocán Glas agus ar an Tuar Beag. Tá a gcuid deirfiuracha siúd – Máire i gCathair na Gaillimhe, Bríd i gCo na Mí and Eibhlín i Sligeach. Agus is col cúigir do John Ford í Nora Ní Chonghaile (Uí Chualáin) nó Nóra Mhikeen atá ina cónaí ar an gCoill Rua. Ba le Nóra an seál a chaith Maureen O'Hara sa scannán agus tá an seál céanna coinnigh slán sábhailte ag Nóra i gcónaí. Chomh maith leis sin thug Nóra cúnamh do Mhaureen O'Hara agus í ag déanamh "faoistine" as Gaeilge sa scannán. Bhí páirteanna "extras" ag Máire and Bríd Ní Fheinneadha sa scannán agus ag Nóra Mhikeen agus thagadh carr dhá n-iarradh chuile mhaidin ar feadh sé seachtainí an Samhradh sin le iad a thabhairt go Conga i gcomhair na scannánaíochta.

Ba as an Spidéal freisin ar ndóigh do Mhicheál Morris nó "Lord Killanin" mar ab fhearr aithne air. Deireadh seisean i gcónaí go raibh gaol idir a mhuintir féin agus muintir Uí Fheinneadha. Ba uncail leis a d'fhág athair John Ford, Seán Mháire, thíos i gCóbh Chorcaí nuair a bhí sé ag dul go Meiriceá. Chuir Killanin aithne i dtosach ar Ford nuair a thug sé cuairt ar Los Angeles ar a bhealach ar ais ón tSín, áit a raibh sé ag tuairisciú don *Daily Mail* ar an gcogadh idir an tSín agus an tSeapáin i ndeireadh na dtriochaidí. Nuair a tháinig Ford go hÉirinn thug Killanin thart ar fud Chonamara agus deisceart Mhaigh Eo é go bhfeicfeadh sé na radharcanna breátha agus bhí sé ráite go raibh fonn ar Ford cuid den scannán a dhéanamh thart ar theach mór an Spidéil ach nach raibh baileach a ndóthain fairsinge acu ann agus chomh maith leis sin nach raibh aon Óstán sách mór sa cheantar don fhoireann ollmhór a bhí ag obair ar an scannán agus a bheadh ag fanacht sa chomharsanacht.

Ní féidir dearmad a dhéanamh ach oiread ar Mháirtín Ó Droighneáin – Máirtín Thornton an dornálaí. Bhain Máirtín Craobh na hÉireann amach i 1944 agus ba mhór é a cháil fós seacht mbliana ina dhiaidh sin. Bhí beagán gaoil idir Máirtín agus John Ford agus féach gur Thornton an sloinne a tugadh ar an bpríomhcharactar sa scannán i.e. Seán Thornton an pháirt a rinne John Wayne. Ba dornálaí a bhí i Seán Thornton freisin d'réir scéil an scannáin. Bhí baint ag Máirtín Ó Droighneáin leis an troid a bhí sa scannán idir Seán Thorton agus Red Will Danaher. Fuaim dhornaí Mháirtín atá le cloisteáil sa scannán. Dúirt Joe Mellotte, fear a sheas isteach do John Wayne sa scannán ó am go ham, dúirt sé liom gur iarr Máirtín Thornton John Wayne amach ar an "bhfair play" oíche an lae ar chríochnaigh an scannán. Dúirt sé go raibh píosa breá troda eatarthu agus neart dornaí á gcaitheamh ar chaon taobh. Bhí cáil an "tough guy" ar John Wayne an uair sin i ngeall ar na scannáin agus is dóigh go raibh Thornton ag iarraidh beagán gaoithe a bhaint as a chuid seolta. Dúirt Joe Mellotte freisin gur ól Wayne buidéal fuisce ar an Mám an lá ar chríochnaigh an scannánaíocht, sa teach ósta atá ag Joe Keane ann inniú.

Ar ndóigh bhí Droighneáin eile ar an Tuar Beag comharsain béal dorais le muintir Uí Fheinneadha a ghlac páirt mhór sa troid in aghaidh na Tans in gcogadh na saoirse. Go deimhin dódh an teach cúpla babhta ortha. B'shin iad muintir Sheáin Mhicil – Joe, Dan agus Mícheál. Bhí aithne agam féin ar Mhícheál mar bhí sé ina Phríomh Oide i scoil náisiúnta na bhForbacha le linn dom freastal ar an scoil sin i dtús na gcaogadaí. Tháinig Ford abhaile go hÉirinn i 1921 agus chonaic sé an obair a bhí ar bun ag na Tans. Bhí sé ráite go raibh clampar idir é féin agus iad féin istigh i mbaile mór na Gaillimhe lá agus gur thóg siad é, ach gur ligeadar leis nuair a fuaireadar amach go mba saoránach Meiriceánach a bhí ann. Bhí Ford go mór ar shon saoirse na hÉireann agus is cinnte go raibh fíor mheas aige ar na Droighneáin. Go deimhin thiocfadh dhó go raibh baint aige sin le gur thug sé an sloinne Thornton ar character John Wayne sa scannán.

Agus ní féidir dearmad a dhéanamh ar Mhicheál Ó Briain as an gCoileach a rinne mionpháirt sa scannán. Chaith Micheál blianta fada ina aisteoir in Amharclann na Mainistreach i mBaile Átha Cliath – fearacht go leor aisteoirí eile a bhí sa scannán – Barry Fitzgerald agus a dheartháir Arthur Shields (throid Arthur in éirí amach na

Cásca), May Craig, Eileen Crowe, Seán McClory as Gaillimh, Eric Gorman, Joseph O'Dea (deartháir le Jimmy O'Dea) agus Jack MacGowran a rinne a gcuid páirteanna chomh paitianta sin san *Quiet Man*. Rinne McClory aisteoireacht le Taibhdhearc na Gaillimhe freisin agus is fiú a lua gurbh iad cantóirí na Taibhdheirce a chloistear sa scannán ag canadh *The Wild Colonial Boy* agus amhráin eile a chantar istigh tí "Phat Cohan".

Faoi láthair tá Telegael, comhlacht físe sa Spidéal i mbun pleanála le leagan Gaeilge den scannán a dhéanamh. Is fiú a lua go raibh beagán Gaeilge ag John Ford agus go ndearna sé iarracht í a labhairt go háirithe agus é ag scannánaíocht. In agallamh a rinne an dornálaí Máirtín Ó Droighneáin liom do Raidio na Gaeltachta in 1973 dúirt sé go mbíodh Ford ag fógairt air féin as Gaeilge nuair a bhíodh sé ag dornálaíocht sa scannán – "an dorna a Mháirtín, an dorna, tabhair an dorna dhó". Thaitnigh an ceol Gaelach le Ford freisin go háirithe agus é casta ar an mbosca ceoil agus déarfadh sé as Gaeilge ar an seit "cáil an ceoltóir, cáil an ceoltóir".

Tá sé i gceist go mbeadh teacht le chéile de Mhuintir Uí Fheinneadha i gCois Fharraige i Mí Mheán Fómhair. Tá sé i gceist go dtiocfadh cuid de ghaolta Ford i gceantar Maine agus St. Paul agus in áiteanna eile ar fud Mheiriceá abhaile i gcomhair na hócáide. Táthar ag súil go mbeidh an leagan Gaeilge den scannán réidh don cheiliúradh speisialta sin. Bheadh Ford féin sásta leis sin cheapfainn.

(English summary translation on page 165)

Maura (Burke) Byrne

I am sending on a few miserable snaps which I took in Cong. Etta Vaughan who was Maureen O'Hara's stand-in, was a friend of my sister's Kathleen Burke. Etta invited us to meet the cast of *The Quiet Man* on one of the days when filming was suspended due to weather problems.

I remember that my mother was hoping we would model our hairstyles on Maureen O'Hara – just in case!!

We met Maureen O'Hara, John Wayne, Barry Fitzgerald and Victor McLaglen in the lounge of Ashford Castle. Although I was fifteen years of age, I do not remember being overawed in any way – weren't we lucky that it was in the days before *Hello* magazine etc.!

Later in the evening, filming resumed and we went out on to the streets, where we were able to ramble around, as the stars did their various takes. We took part in one of the crowd scenes, but I have never been able to identify myself!

The few snaps I have were taken rather unprofessionally by a box camera. I hope they can be of some use to you.

Looking forward to your book,
Yours Sincerely,
Maura (Burke) Byrne.

O'Hara and Wayne pose near White O'Morn.

Chapter Eleven

And so Farewell

Those of us who watch *The Quiet Man* again and again on video and DVD come to believe that the stars, like the characters they portray are immortal. Sadly, they are not, and since the appearance of CGQM several people connected with the movie have gone to their eternal reward. Here we pay tribute to some of them.

The beautiful Kylemore Abbey, Connemara, near which many Quiet Man scenes were shot.

ETTA VAUGHAN

During the shooting of *The Quiet Man*, a young lady called Etta Vaughan, who lived in the village of Moycullen near Galway, decided to have afternoon tea at Ashford Castle to see all the stars at close quarters. First Assistant Director and John Ford's brother-in-law Wingate Smith spotted the lovely, slim and red-haired Etta and realising that her height and figure were very similar to Maureen O'Hara's, offered her the job of stand-in and double on the spot. He was amazed that she had to consult her mother before accepting and even then she was not allowed to stay in Cong but was ferried in and out to Galway each day in a limousine.

Etta Vaughan, Stand-in and double for Maureen O'Hara, with Maureen, Webb Overlander and other extras in Cong.

Etta Vaughan, who had been chosen over a hundred other girls who had applied for the job, acted as Maureen's stand-in throughout the entire shooting in Ireland. She also appeared as Maureen's double in at least three scenes – the pony trap ride by Kylemore Abbey, the entry to Clifden, and Mary Kate's sudden departure from the cattle fair. For her trouble she received £60 a week, a veritable fortune for a young woman in 1951.

The author had the pleasure of meeting Etta Vaughan in 2001 when we acted as two of the judges in the Mary Kate Danaher look-alike competition. She was a truly delightful lady, kind and gentle, and full of memories about the movie. She got to know and like all of the cast members and they were very kind to her. Ford, whether jokingly or not, suggested that she might go to

Maureen O'Hara and her stand-in Etta Vaughan relax at Ashford Farm between takes.

Winners of the Mary Kate Danaher and Sean Thornton lookalike competition, Doreen Byrne of Dublin and Peter MacIntyre of Glasgow. The competition was judged by Etta Vaughan and the author.

Hollywood to seek work in the movie industry, but she declined. Later she travelled widely, living in Malaysia, Paris and London before returning to settle down in Galway. Here she married Bernard O'Sullivan of the family who owned the car driven by Mr. Playfair in *The Quiet Man*.

On Monday March 8th 2002, at 8.15 in the evening, the 87-year-old Etta O'Sullivan was crossing the road in Galway city when she was knocked down by a car. She died from her injuries soon afterwards. Etta was a deeply religious lady, always in good spirits and very active – in fact she had booked a trip to Italy shortly before her fatal accident. She will live forever on screen in *The Quiet Man* and may her gentle soul rest in peace.

SEAN McCLORY

Another *Quiet Man* star, Sean McClory, died in Hollywood on December 10th 2003, aged 79. Sean was born in Galway on March 8th 1924, where his father was a councillor. After a few years studying medicine at University College Galway, where he gained theatrical experience, he decided he did not want to be a doctor and, when his family moved to Dublin, he joined Dublin's Abbey Theatre where he developed as a fine actor. In the late nineteen forties, he took the Hollywood trail and in a long and successful career spanning almost fifty years he appeared in more than a hundred films and television shows.

Sometimes credited as Sean McGlory, which Americans found easier to pronounce, he appeared in several Dick Tracy movies before his first breakthrough in *Roughshod* (1949). He got on well with Ford and landed the part of the pipe-smoking IRA gentleman Owen Glynn in *The Quiet Man*. He did not come to Ireland for the location shots and there is a lot of speculation why, but in the event this fact turned out to be useful as his character is a marker for scenes shot in the studio.

In time Sean McClory was proud to become a member of the Ford "stock company" as a prominent supporting actor, starring in Ford films such as *What Price Glory* (1952), *The Long Gray Line* (1955) and *Cheyenne Autumn* (1964). He often played hard drinking Irishmen such as Dublin O'Malley in Mickey Spillane's *Ring of Fear* (1954) but he was by no means restricted to such roles – for example he appeared in *David and Bathsheba* (1951) and *Les Misérables* (1952).

In later years he appeared mostly in television series such as *Rawhide*, *The Outer Limits* and *Bring 'Em Back Alive*. One of his last appearances was in James Joyce's *The Dead* (1987) directed by John Huston, which Ford had planned to include as the fourth leaf of his shamrock in *The Rising of the Moon* (1957).

Etta Vaughan in later life - still a lovely lady.

"Where will I put it?" Michaeleen (Barry Fitzgerald) embarrasses Mary Kate Danaher (Maureen O'Hara) with a pointed question regarding the filling of the cradle. Sean Thornton (John Wayne) waits for an answer. In the centre is Owen Glynn (Sean McClory) and on his left is Hugh Forbes, (Charles Fitzsimons) Maureen's brother).

The Wayne family in costumes by O'Máille's *of Galway. (l to r) Toni, Patrick, Duke, Melinda and Michael.*

McClory spent nearly eight weeks in Hollywood on set when the interior scenes were shot and, in a series of interviews with Jordan R. Young, talked about what happened then.

"We rehearsed scenes as they were written but by the time we shot them, they were different. They were much improved, stamped with Ford's own personal touch. Off the set, I assure you that there was not a sober breath drawn in all that time. But we were never drunk on the set – Ford was a stickler for that".

Jack MacGowran and Sean McClory were notorious drinking partners – perhaps that is one reason why Ford did not want them together in Ireland. In later years McGlory did return to Ireland for several *Quiet Man* events and often expressed the usual emigrant's wish to return home for good. His kindly soul now rests in the United States.

MICHAEL WAYNE

In 1993 I attended the celebrations to mark the opening of the Archive at the Film Institute of Ireland in Dublin and also the tenth anniversary of the founding of that organisation. The plaque unveiled read;

1993

Major support for the Archive was received from The Los Angeles Chapter of the American Ireland fund. In tribute to Maureen O'Hara and John Wayne for their performance together in The Quiet Man.

After the showing of the movie (guess which one!) that evening, I joined the many hundreds of fans who queued to talk with and obtain autographs from Michael Wayne, Duke Wayne's eldest son. He was a very patient and good-humoured man and we discussed the film for several minutes giving various reasons why it had become so popular. Michael had himself appeared in several scenes – as the altar boy and beside Father Lonergan asking the crowd to cheer like good Protestants, for example, and had very fond memories of Cong and Ireland.

Imagine my shock in April 2003, a mere ten years later, on opening my newspaper to find that he had died at the relatively early age of 68. He was born Michael Anthony Morrison to John Wayne and his first wife Josephine Saenz in 1934. After graduating from Loyola University, California and serving in the US Air Force Reserve, Michael Wayne worked for his father's production company Batjac and was production assistant on *The Alamo* (1960) which went disastrously over budget. Becoming head of Batjac a year later, Michael eventually turned the huge losses on this movie into a profit with television releases and reissues. His very careful handling of the company's finances eventually ensured its financial viability. At twenty-five he produced *McLintock!* (1963) starring Wayne and O'Hara and the movie made $4 million at the box office. Further productions included *The Green Berets* (1968), *Chisum* (1970) and *The Train Robbers* (1973).

After his father's death in 1979, Michael Wayne very carefully controlled the rate of re-release of movies starring Duke Wayne to television and the cinema. The result was that they were eagerly awaited and never taken for granted and virtually every video or DVD outlet in the world today carries Wayne movies in their dozens. Television stations worldwide show Wayne movies continuously, in particular BBC1, Sky Cinema and Turner Classic Movies.

Michael Wayne was a courteous gentleman as well as being a shrewd businessman largely responsible for Duke's current worldwide popularity. May his noble soul rest in peace.

James Lilburn (Father Paul), Michael Wayne, Patrick Wayne (extras) and Feeney (Jack MacGowran) take time out on Lettergesh Beach at the races.

Chapter Twelve

What John Ford Thought of The Quiet Man

John Ford was a modest man. He liked to pretend that he was just a routine film-maker. "I'm John Ford, I make Westerns", he used to say simply about his work and his huge output. *The Quiet Man* was his tribute to the land of his ancestors and he tried to pass it off as just another job of work, but he knew it was pretty good and deep down he was as proud as punch about it. In his peculiar Fordean way, he never would admit that of course, but just a few times, mostly in interviews, he let his guard drop and inadvertently revealed his true feelings about what was undoubtedly one of his favourite movies. Here are some of the things he let slip.

Director John Ford in Cong shows the camera crew how it's done!

1. *The Quiet Man* was one of the best, especially because of the Irish climate. I made it in my home, in my country. All the extras were friends of the family. We shot it among friends. That's how I like to work. I hate affectation. You do your job, that's all. Sometimes it's good, sometimes it's less good, sometimes it's a failure. It happens to everyone.

2. Hey, *The Quiet Man* looks pretty good. Everybody here is enthused and I even like it myself. It has a strange humorous quality and the mature romance comes off well. I am now in the throes of cutting, dubbing music – that is indeed the tough part, requiring meticulous attention to detail. I think the Irish might even like it…

3. *The Quiet Man* looks better every day.

4. The first "motion" pictures were Leland Stanford's photos of a running horse. For your information a running horse remains the finest subject for a motion-picture camera.

5. Now, I'm a Roman Catholic. But, I'm Irish too. I think I'm fairly masculine and I don't think I'm a prude, but I do think there are certain things that don't belong on the screen. I wouldn't take anyone to see some of the pictures that are being put out today. I wouldn't even take them to see the billboards outside of the movie houses. These and other ads, lurid come-ons with half-naked women, are dishonest and cater to our worst instincts.

Duke Wayne, John Ford and Arthur Shields (Rev. Mr. Playfair) stride out from Galway to Mayo across the bridge at Ashford Castle.

They aren't making Hollywood any friends.

Ford the director with a friendly dog in Cong.

6. Actually, I'm certainly not against sex on the screen if it is done in the right way. Many Westerns have a gutsy sort of sex. And I think I made the sexiest picture ever, *The Quiet Man*. Now this was all about a man trying to get a woman into bed, but that was alright, they were married, and it was essentially a moral situation done with honesty, good taste and humour.

These things are all fundamental to a good Western, too. In a Western you can make a strong picture which is reasonably adult, yet a man can still take his children to see it, which is the way it should be. After all, we're not in the burlesque business.

7. *The Quiet Man* is a very sexy story, you know. I like good lusty sex but I object to dirty innuendoes. The customs shown in *The Quiet Man* are true and prevail in Connemara which is the poorest country in Ireland and the only one Cromwell never conquered. I was born in Cape Elizabeth, Maine, but I went to school in Ireland for a while and was brought up to speak both English and Gaelic. Every Irishman is an actor. The Irish and the coloured people are the most natural actors in the world.

The Quiet Man was photographed in the rain – or Irish Mist, as they call it in Ireland. That helped the picture a lot.

8. We had a lot of preparation on the script of *The Quiet Man*, laid out the story pretty carefully, but in such a way that if any chance for comedy came up we could put it in – like Barry Fitzgerald bringing the crib into their bedroom on the morning after the wedding night and seeing the broken bed. That was just taking advantage of the situation. Nobody has ever heard what he says when he comes in there, you know – because the laugh is too loud. Hundreds of people have asked me – "what did he say?" I never can figure it out ["Impetuous – Homeric"]. But that condition still exists in Connemara – where my

John Ford with friend Lord Killanin at Ashford.

John Ford relaxes with a friend on a footpath in Cong.

people came from – the wife is supposed to come to her husband with a "dot" or dowry – a few pounds or something – it's a good thing.

Mary Kate's feelings in the film were just good drama. The only mistake we made was having him throw the money on the fire – he should have tossed it to one of the fellows and said, "Give it to charity" or something. But whom would he give it to anyway? Not the Parish Priest – he has more money than the Lord Mayor of Dublin.

9. Yes, I like *The Quiet Man*. There again I had trouble with Herb Yates. He kept complaining, "It's all green. Don't they have any browns or blacks in Ireland? Why does it have to be all green?" I had a lot of fun with old Herb on that one. He wanted to call it *The Prizefighter and the Colleen*. I felt that was an awful title because it tipped the story that Duke Wayne was a boxer. Well, Yates said that he received lots of letters from exhibitors who told him that they preferred his title to *The Quiet Man*. I asked to look at the letters, and he showed them to me. "What a strange coincidence!" I told him. "All these letters have the same date and say the same thing". Obviously he had sent out a letter that was practically mimeographed and asked the theatre men to write in letters. And they did. But I still wouldn't go with his title.

10. *The Quiet Man* was made in my mother's and father's country, Connemara, Ireland. It was a lot of fun doing the picture. We got breaks on the weather, and when the weather wasn't particularly good, we still went out and took advantage of the bad weather. When the picture was shown in Ireland, all the critics were angry. They didn't like it. Every one of them came up with the same statement – that Mr. Ford had used a green filter on his camera to make the hills and fields green. I really blew my top at them, and I had to laugh. I'd never heard of a green filter, and you can't use a filter on a Technicolor camera anyway. So I wrote each one of the critics a nice letter saying if you would get out of that goddamn apartment and take a bus ride into the country, you would see that the hills of Northern Ireland are green. But these stupid guys, these city dwellers living in Dublin, saying that I used a green filter – that really got my goat.

John Ford seeks peace and quiet in Cong, caught unawares.

11. *The Quiet Man* is a lovely story and I think we should go all over Ireland and get a bit of scenery here and a bit of scenery there and really make the thing a beautiful travelogue, besides a really charming story.

SOURCES
1. Interview with Jean Mitry (1955) in *Cinemonde.*
2. Correspondence with Lord Killanin (October 1951)
3. Ibid.
4. Interview with *Newsweek* (1958)
5. Interview with Bill Libby (1964)
6. Ibid.
7. Interview with George J. Mitchell, (1964) *Films In Review*
8. *Searching for John Ford,* Joseph McBride St. Martins Press (2001)
9. Interview with Burt Kennedy, *Actor Magazine* (1968)
10. Interview with Walter Wagner (1973)
11.Screenplay Instructions to Frank Nugent

Wayne, Ford and Fitzgerald leave for Ireland to shoot The Quiet Man.

Chapter Thirteen

The Quiet Man of Inisfree

I will arise and go now, by train to Inisfree
And a pretty cottage buy there where I was born;
Nine rose bushes will I plant there
And live with Mary Kate at White O'Morn.

I am a quiet man and in my dreams have not forgotten
The brooks and fords of Cong and Teernakill.
With Michaeleen by my side I'll win the Inisfree Cup
And in Cohan's Bar my friends will drink their fill.

On a tandem Mary Kate and I will roam through Galway
And stretch my legs walking home from Castletown.
But I must first fight Red Will in a field of hay
And plunge him in the river 'til he's had enough.

Then peace and quiet will at last come to Inisfree
And the flocks of Lonergan and Playfair
Will live in quiet Homeric harmony
And Mary Kate will whisper secrets in my ear.

Des MacHale 2001

Chapter Fourteen

What Happened Next? A Sequel to The Quiet Man

Mary Kate whispered something in her husband Sean Thornton's ear – what it was it seems no one will ever know, but we can guess that it may have been a romantic suggestion at very least! Then she threw away the fine stick that was never actually used to beat the lovely lady and bounded on to the stepping stones over the brook, turning to look back at her husband when she reached the other side. He smiled and followed her eagerly, but she coyly ran ahead and waited for him to catch up with her. She tried to break away from his grasp, but this time he did not let go, so, like a pair of love-stuck teenagers they strolled up the lane together towards White O'Morning. That was the very lane that Sean had walked down sadly with another woman – his mother – many years ago as they began their journey to the New World. Now Sean and Mary Kate were beginning a new life together as man and wife, and they lived happily ever after.

Or did they? Well, in the immortal words of Michaeleen Óg Flynn, they did and they didn't. Like most married couples, they had their ups and downs. Sean became a gentleman farmer – there wasn't a great deal of evidence of potatoes or turnips or cabbage about the place. He hunted, he fished, he shot game with an old gun, and of course he rode through the fields on that black hunter of his, at times whooping for joy with the sheer exhilaration of his happy lifestyle.

Mary Kate too was as blissfully happy at White O'Morning as May Thornton had been before her – taking delight in cooking, housework and the odd shopping trip to Castletown in her one horsepower vehicle. She kept a few hens and chickens about the homestead and there were always fresh eggs available as well as roast chicken and soup for special occasions. Sometimes Sean would bring home to her a bundle of second-hand American magazines, full of ideas for décor and fashion that she loved to look at even if there was little hope in reality of achieving such standards in Inisfree. Sean hired a grand little girl called Mary, a grandniece of Dan Tobin's, from the village to help out his wife and soon the girl's presence became absolutely necessary because Mary Kate Thornton was forbidden to lift any heavy weights for the most natural of reasons.

Sean was thrilled at the prospect of becoming a father and the couple's first child was born almost a year to the day after they were married. It was a bit disappointing that the little lad didn't have red hair like his mother but what matter, there was still lots of time for that. Naturally, they called him Michael after his grandfather and he soon became known as Young Mike Thornton. Two years later Mary Kate and Sean had a beautiful red-haired daughter whom they named Mary Kate Sarah. Just how happy can a couple get?

White O'Morning became quite a social centre. Hugh Forbes and Owen Glynn were regular visitors and for them the decanter of whiskey was always produced. Another frequent visitor was Michaeleen Óg Flynn but he preferred the bottle, and still persisted in his quaint habit of throwing away the cork just in case it might ever be used again. Michaeleen was now a sad figure confined to a wheelchair, often pushed from place to place by Father Lonergan, but he was always in good spirits literally and figuratively. From time to time the Playfairs too dropped by, mostly by car but occasionally on the tandem; the ploy with the bishop worked like a charm and the Playfairs were left in Inisfree for the remainder of their ecclesiastical careers and lived in retirement there too as they had wished for devoutly.

But the most welcome guests of all at White

Michaeleen Óg Flynn (Barry Fitzgerald) supervises the courting of Red Will Danaher (Victor McLaglen) and the Widow Tillane (Mildred Natwick) on the streets of Inisfree.

O'Morning were Squire William Danaher and his lovely bride Sarah. Soon after the big fight their courtship began under the watchful eye of Michaeleen and after a few heavy sessions of patty fingers, Red Will popped the question to his beloved Widow Tillane. This time he made sure there were no big ears around with pipes in their mouths and pints in their fists to hear his proposal and this time Sarah was keen to name the happy day. It was of course a mixed Protestant-Catholic marriage performed jointly by Mister Playfair and Father Lonergan in keeping with the ecumenical tradition of Inisfree. The celebrations went on for days and even Old Dan Tobin, miraculously restored to full health by the big fight, took an active part in the singing, dancing and drinking.

At the reception, Red Will Danaher was to drop a bombshell. At one stage in the proceedings he made his usual call to Pat Cohan (still going strong) to fill up the glasses, saying "I've got a little announcement to make". There was a hush. What was the ex-bully boy of Inisfree going to say now? Would it lead to another big fight, and between whom? Even Michaeleen, sipping a pint of porter in his wheelchair, began to wonder if he should resume his career as village bookmaker.

With glass in hand, Red Will beamed as he addressed the guests including Mary Kate and Sean, Father Lonergan, Feeney, Cyril and Elizabeth Playfair, Hugh Forbes and Owen Glynn, Father Paul (now parish priest himself in Ballinrobe), Dan Tobin and Michaeleen Óg Flynn. "Sarah darling and I are a bit too advanced in years", he told them, "to be thinking of starting a family", and there were smiles and peals of laughter all round from the assembled guests. "But we don't need to," he continued, "because we already have a family". There was a stunned silence throughout the reception room – Mary Kate blushed to the roots of her red hair and Mrs. Playfair had to be helped to a chair. "And let me introduce our son to you", beamed Red Will, holding his wife Sarah's hand all the time. The suspense was killing as he paused and pointed to one Ignatius Feeney. There were gasps of amazement from the guests as poor old Feeney promptly fainted and had to be revived on the floor by a glass of brandy, just about the only free drink he ever received from Red Will Danaher.

What had happened was this, and it took a long time for the story to emerge. In their youth, Red Will and Sarah had fallen in love, but because she was a Protestant and he was a Catholic and neither of their parents would allow them to convert, marriage was out of the question, things not being as liberal then as they are now. Sarah was shipped off to an exclusive boarding school in the South of England (hence her accent) to keep her out of harm's way. But true love will find a way and soon Red Will followed his beloved to England and they resumed their courtship in secret. Soon Sarah was expecting their child but she never told anyone – neither Red Will nor her parents. She gave birth to the baby – a strapping boy – in England and he was immediately given up for adoption. Sarah thought that she had put her past behind her and that she would never see her son again.

Later she returned home to Inisfree where even the all-knowing Father Lonergan believed that she had neither chick nor child, poor soul! Relations with Red Will were decidedly cool and he couldn't understand why. Within a few years, her parents married her off to a wealthy landowner, Jasper Tillane, with whom she lived contentedly if not happily for many years. When he died, he left her a fortune in land and money, and she assumed a respectable existence as the merry widow Tillane. But Red Will had a suspicious nature – where had his Sarah disappeared to for several months all those years ago? He hired a private detective who ferreted out the whole story. Feeney's adopted parents had both died so Red Will decided to foster the lad and bring him home to Ireland passing him off as a personal assistant. Only Red Will knew who he was – Sarah knew nothing and Feeney never suspected a thing. Nobody in Inisfree knew what the situation was either, with the possible exception of Michaeleen Óg Flynn, who knew almost everything, but in this case he wisely kept his mouth shut.

In the years that followed Mary Kate and Sean had several other children, ten in all. There was a great deal of tension over land, money and inheritance, between the descendants of the Danahers and the descendants of the Thorntons. Young Mike Thornton held that Squire Ignatius Feeney-Danaher, as he grandly styled himself, was not the legitimate heir to the Danaher-Tillane estate, and that the property should revert to him through his mother Mary Kate Thornton, née Danaher. So he challenged Feeney to a duel and there was another big fight in Inisfree. But that's another story…

The twist in the tale – is Feeney (Jack MacGowran) the true heir to the Danaher/Thornton lands and fortune?

Scenes from the Film

A helping hand – gangway. Sean and Mary Kate with Owen Glynn (Sean McClory) and Hugh Forbes (Charles Fitzsimons) at (the American) White O'Morn.

Above: How did you sleep? Don't be shaming me in front of your friends.
Below: O'Hara and Wayne pose near White O'Morn.

Father Paul (James Lilburn) and Father Lonergan (Ward Bond) watch the big fight at Inisfree.

Dancing partners - just before the first kiss in the cottage.

Mary Kate Danaher (Maureen O'Hara) and Sean Thorntion (John Wayne) move her furniture into the (American) White O'Morn.

Duke Wayne and Maureen O'Hara share a joke on Ashford Farm.

Sean (John Wayne) and Mary Kate (Maureen O'Hara) cross the brook in their one horse-power vehicle in front of White O'Morn.

At length the couple have escaped on the tandem in front of the Playfair House.

A bicycle made for two.

Mr. Thornton, meet Miss Danaher.

"Let the courting commence". Mary Kate Danaher (Maureen O'Hara), Father Lonergan (Ward Bond), Red Will Danaher (Victor McLaglen), Father Paul (James Lilburn) and Sean Thornton (John Wayne), on the Ashford Farm near Cong.

The happily-married couple in the doorway of (the American) White O'Morn.

A rosy cheek!

Pattyfingers in the Holy Water – filmed outside the Ashford Church of Ireland.

And so they were married – the wedding photograph.

Mary Kate Danaher (Mary O'Hara) and Sean Thornton (John Wayne) say goodbye to movie-viewers near the (Irish) White O'Morn.

Let's go home Mary Kate - just before the fight at the wedding.

Sean Thornton (John Wayne) and Red Will Danaher shake hands in Cohan's Bar with, left to right, Frank Baker, Barry Fitzgerald, Sean McClory, Colin Kenny, Charles Fitzsimons, James Lilburn and Jack MacGowran in close attendance.

A dash for freedom and the tandem.

Translation

The Quiet Man By Mike P. O' Conaola

The Quiet Man was made in 1951 and has become the most famous Irish Film. Thousands of tourists come to the west of Ireland every summer to see the locations - Ashford Castle, Ballyglunin, Maam, Leam Bridge and of course Cong. Other places such as Spiddal, home of director John Ford's father are also important. From there John Feeney emigrated to Portland, Maine in 1872. Here he met his future wife Barbara Curran - although they had lived only a few miles away from each other in Ireland they never met until they went to the United States. Here they married and raised twelve children, of whom John Aloysius Feeney (John Ford) was the youngest. The walls of the original house still stand in Connemara. Many of Ford's relations still live in Spiddal. One cousin, Nora, owned the shawl that Maureen O'Hara wore in the film and still keeps it safely. Nora also helped Noreen with her confessions in Irish in the movie. Two other cousins, Maire and Brid, were extras and were ferried to Cong every morning by motor car. Lord Killanin was also connected with Spiddal and was also in fact a relation of the Feeneys - it was his uncle who left John Ford's father in Cobh on his way to America. Killanin met Ford in Los Angeles and later showed all the beautiful sights of Connemara and south Mayo that are shown in the film. It is said that Ford wanted to use Spiddal as a location in the film but the area lacked suitable accomodation. We must not forget Martin Thornton the boxer, all Ireland champion in 1944 and a distant relation of Ford's. The name of the boxer in the film was Thornton after him. On the final night of filming Thornton challenged Wayne to a real fight to put the Hollywood tough guy in his place. They ended up drinking a bottle of whiskey together in Joe Keane's pub in Maam. Other Thornton cousins - Joe, Dan and Michael, took an active part in the war against the Black and Tans and had their home burnt down as a consequence. John Ford came to Ireland in 1921 - protesting at what had been done, he was arrested in Galway but was released when they discovered he was an American citizen. Ford was very interested in Irish independence, and had a great respect for the Thornton's part in it. We remember another Connemara-man Michael O' Brien who had another small part in the film. He was an Abbey Theatre actor as were Barry Fitzgerald, his brother Arthur Shields (he fought in the 1916 Rising) May Craig, Eileen Crowe, Galway man Sean McClory, Eric Gorman, Joseph O' Dea and Jack McGowran. Galway actors from the Taibhdhearc Theatre provided musical accompaniment. At present, Telegael, a TV company based in Spiddal plan to make a version of the Quiet Man in Irish. Ford had a little Irish and used to use it during filming egging on Martin Thornton with "Box him Martin, give it to him" in Irish. Ford also loved Irish music especially the melodian and used to call out in Irish "Praise the musician!" It is hoped to have a gathering of the Feeney clan next September and it is planned to have the American cousins there too when the Irish Quiet Man is ready. Ford would surely have approved.

Time out for two mugs of tea at Ashford.